Andrew Marvell

Andrew Marvell

POET & POLITICIAN
1621 – 78

An exhibition
to commemorate the
tercentenary of
his death

British Library Reference Division
14 *July*–1 *October* 1978

Catalogue compiled by
Hilton Kelliher

=

Published for
THE BRITISH LIBRARY
by
British Museum Publications Limited

© 1978 The British Library Board
ISBN 0 7141 0394 2 *paper*
    0 7141 0395 0 *cased*

Published by British Museum Publications Ltd
6 Bedford Square, London WC1B 3RA

Designed by Brian Paine
Set in Monophoto Ehrhardt 453
and printed in Great Britain by
Jolly and Barber Ltd, Rugby, Warwickshire

Cover and frontispiece: Portrait of Andrew Marvell
c. 1657–62 (National Portrait Gallery)

British Library Cataloguing in Publication Data

Kelliher, William Hilton
   Andrew Marvell.
    1. Marvell, Andrew – Bibliography
    2. Marvell, Andrew – Exhibitions
    3. British Library. Reference Division
    I. Title   II. British Library. Reference Division
    016.821'4   Z8551.6/

Contents

Foreword

THE plan of the present catalogue follows with only two exceptions that of the chapters in the late Pierre Legouis' *Andrew Marvell* (Oxford, 2nd edn., 1968), which is itself a distillation, incorporating the fruits of subsequent researches, of the same scholar's still unsurpassed study entitled *André Marvell: poete, puritain, patriote* (Paris and Oxford, 1928). For many of the statements made in the following pages precise references are to be traced in either the French work or its English counterpart, or else in the expanded commentary to H. M. Margoliouth's edition of *The Poems and Letters of Andrew Marvell* (Oxford, 3rd edn., rev. by Pierre Legouis and E. E. Duncan-Jones, 1971). No consistent attempt has been made to provide a bibliography for the individual items: such references as appear in the catalogue are confined largely to sources not available to or not sufficiently exploited by these scholars.

Some of the new material that appears in the exhibition and catalogue, notably items 17, 18, 20, and 57–61, will be discussed by Mrs Pauline Burdon and the compiler in two articles to be published in separate issues of the *British Library Journal* this year.

The text and titles of poems quoted in the catalogue are taken from the earliest printed versions unless otherwise stated, or where (as in the case of 'The Last Instructions') a manuscript source has been used. Very occasionally (as with the 'Horatian *Ode*', l.31, and *Upon Appleton House*, l.328, where the Folio reads 'hightest' and 'The' respectively) obvious errors have been emended. In quotations from manuscript common contractions have often been silently expanded, while spelling and punctuation remain as in the original. Finally, all manuscript-numbers and press-marks of printed books not otherwise distinguished are from the collections of the British Library.

As part of the extended celebrations that are planned for the tercentenary of Marvell's death, a selection of items from the present exhibition, together with some from elsewhere, will go on display in the Brynmor Jones Library of the University of Hull between 16 October and 25 November 1978, under the title 'Andrew Marvell as a Writer'.

Acknowledgements

The British Library Board wishes to thank those institutions and individuals who have generously lent to this exhibition: Lady Anne Bentinck (83B, C, D; 79, 100). The Trustees of the Bedford Estates (107). The Curators of the Bodleian Library (37–39, 41, 52, 58, 61, 82, 85). Cambridge University Archives (8, 13). Department of Coins and Medals, British Museum (55, 89: see also 48). The Department of Medieval and Later Antiquities, British Museum (53). The Department of Prints and Drawings, British Museum (24, 27, 32, 62, 65, 72, 74, 75, 78, 80, 84, 110). His Grace the Duke of Buccleuch and Queensbury (31). The House of Lords Records Office (17). City of Hull Archives (14, 68, 76). Humberside County Record Office (18). Humberside County Libraries: Central Library, Hull (20). The Trustees of the National Portrait Gallery (50, 63). The Vicar of Patrington (1). His Grace the Duke of Portland (83B–D, 79, 100). The Public Record Office (43, 67, 71, 106). The Society of Antiquaries of London (46). T.D.G. Sotheron-Estcourt, Esq. (18).

Photographs in the exhibition and catalogue are reproduced by kind permission of: Lady Anne Bentinck (items 83B, C, D, 100). The Curators of the Bodleian Library (39, 41, 52, 58, 61, 82). The Department of Coins and Medals, British Museum (48, 55, 89). The Department of Prints and Drawings, British Museum (24, 27, 32, 62, 72, 74, 75, 78, 80, 110). British Tourist Authority (p. 27). His Grace the Duke of Buccleuch and Queensbury (31). Cambridge University Archives (8, 13). Harry Cartlidge, Esq. (4, 5). *The Connoisseur* (45). The House of Lords Record Office (17). Hull City Museums and Art Galleries (64). The Warden and Corporation of the Hull Trinity House (81, 83E). Hull University Press (6). Humberside County Record Office (18). Humberside Libraries: Hull Central Library (20). John Lawson, Esq. (6). Leicestershire Record Office (97). The Trustees of the National Portrait Gallery (cover & frontispiece, 50, 63). The Osborn Collection of the Beinecke Rare Book and Manuscript Library, Yale University (88). The Vicar of Patrington (1). The Public Record Office (43, 67, 71, 106, 113). The Vicar of St Giles-in-the-Fields (see 108, 115). M. T. Satterford, Esq. (6). T. D. G. Sotheron-Estcourt, Esq. (18). Trinity College, Cambridge (12, 15).

The compiler wishes particularly to thank the following individuals for help and advice with the catalogue and the exhibition: Bob Aitken, John Barr, John Bradshaw, Pauline Burdon, Vic Carter and the British Library MSS Conservation Section, Harry I. Cartlidge, Joyce Challioner, Jenny Chattington, Warren L. Chernaik, Celia Clear, Timothy Clifford, Harry S. Cobb, Jill Crowther, Alan Dingle, Marie Draper, Susannah Edmunds, Elspeth Evans, Mirjam Foot, J. R. Freeman, Raymond A. Gardner, J. P. W. Gaskell, David and Dorothy Gazey, Richard Green, K. D. Holt, Capt. A. J. C. Hildyard, Hilary Jones, Shelley Jones, Lorna MacEchern, Graham Marsh and the British Library photographers, Brenda Moon, Peter Moore, John Murdoch, Yolande O'Donoghue and the staff of the Map Library, Dorothy Owen, Elaine Paintin, Brian Paine, Pamela Porter, Linda Randall, Jennifer A. Rennie, R. G. Roberts, Malcolm Rogers, E. J. Russell, Robert and Helen Simpson, Cornelia Starks, Linda Stoddart, Hugh Tait, The Rev. G. C. Taylor, Valerie Vaughan, Peter Wheatland, Reg Williams, Sarah Wimbush and The Rev. David Young.

Table of Dates

1621 (31 March) Andrew Marvell born at Winestead in Holderness, Yorkshire.

1624 (20 September) Reverend Andrew Marvell, the poet's father, appointed Master of the Hull Charterhouse.

1629–33 Marvell probably attends Hull Grammar School.

1633 (14 December) Matriculates at Cambridge as sizar of Trinity College: (13 April 1638) elected to a scholarship: (Lent Term 1639) graduates BA.

1641 (23 January) Reverend Marvell drowned: soon after Marvell leaves Cambridge for London, where (February 1642) he lives in Cowcross and witnesses three Savile deeds at Gray's Inn.

1642/3–47 Travels in Holland, France, Italy and Spain, meeting Richard Flecknoe at Rome early in 1646.

1647 (12 November) Sells property in Meldreth, Cambridgeshire, as 'of Kingstone super Hull Gentleman'.

1648 (after 7 July) 'An Elegy upon the Death of my Lord *Francis Villiers*' published, not certainly by Marvell.

1649 (about May) 'To his noble Friend Mr. *Richard Lovelace*' published: (after 24 June) *Upon the Death of the Lord Hastings* published. At this period is assumed to be moving in London literary circles.

1650 (early summer) Writes '*An* Horatian *Ode upon* Cromwell's *Return from* Ireland'. (after 13 November) *Tom May's Death* written, not certainly by Marvell.

1650–2 Tutors Mary Fairfax at Nun Appleton, Yorkshire, and writes the Appleton poems. (winter 1650–1) Composes Latin and English verses to Dr Witty and Latin verses to Oliver St John.

1653 (21 February) Milton recommends him for Latin secretaryship: shortly after writes *The Character of Holland*. (July) Accompanies Cromwell's ward William Dutton to Eton, living in the house of John Oxenbridge. At this time probably composes *Bermudas*, along with 'A Letter to Doctor *Ingelo*' (winter 1653–4) and 'The First Anniversary' (by December 1654).

1656 (about January to August) At Saumur on Loire with William Dutton, where he is described as a 'notable English Italo-Machavellian'.

1657 (spring or summer) Writes '*On the Victory obtained by* Blake *over the* Spaniards'. (September) Appointed Latin Secretary to John Thurloe.

1658   (after 13 April) Composes Latin epitaph for Jane Oxenbridge. (September) Writes the *Poem upon the Death of His late Highness the Lord Protector*. (23 November) Takes part in Cromwell's funeral procession.

1659   (January) Elected joint Member of Parliament for Hull: (May) loses his seat on the restoration of the Rump, at the same time gaining a new superior in Thomas Scott. (about 14 July) Is voted lodgings in Whitehall, probably losing them with his post on the dissolution of the Council of State.

1660   (April) Re-elected Member for Hull.

1662   (June)–1663 (April) Absent in Holland on an unspecified political mission.

1663   (July)–1665 (January) Travels with the Embassy to Russia, Sweden and Denmark as private secretary to the Earl of Carlisle.

1667   (early summer) 'Clarindon's House-Warming' and the early version of 'The Loyall Scot' written. (September) Writes 'The Last Instructions to a Painter'. (October–November) Takes part in the impeachment of Clarendon.

1669   (September) Named in a list of the Duke of York's supporters in the House.

1671   (after May) Writes the epigrams on Blood's attempt on the Crown; and, in the latter half of the year, *Inscribenda Luparae*, distichs on the Louvre.

1672–3 Controversy with Samuel Parker: writes *The Rehearsal Transpros'd*, Part I (autumn 1672) and Part II (early summer 1673).

1674   (summer) Mentioned by Government spies as member of a Dutch fifth-column in England: writes commendatory verses for *Paradise Lost*, 2nd edn. (December) 'Upon his Majesty's being made Free of the City' written.

1675   (April) Writes 'His Majesty's Most Gracious Speech to both Houses of Parliament'. To this year also belong 'The Statue at Charing Cross' and, possibly, 'The Statue in Stocks Market'.

1676   (June) Publishes *Mr. Smirke*, with *A Short Historical Essay on Councils*.

1677   (27 March) Speaks in the House against the Bill to secure the Protestant succession. (June) Takes a house in Great Russell Street in order to conceal two bankrupt friends. (late December) Publishes anonymously *An Account of the Growth of Popery and Arbitrary Government*.

1678   (July) Visits Hull, falling ill on the journey back: (16 August) dies in the house in Great Russell Street and is buried two days later in St Giles-in-the-Fields.

1681   (January) His *Miscellaneous Poems* published by Mary Palmer, alias Marvell.

Early Life

> But as to my Father, he dyed before ever the War broke out,
> having lived with some measure of reputation, both for Piety
> and Learning: and he was moreover a Conformist to the
> established Rites of the Church of *England*, though I confess
> none of the most over-running or eager in them.
>
> *The Rehearsall Transpros'd*, Part II

ANDREW, fourth child of the Reverend Andrew Marvell, a Cambridgeshire man who had held in turn the Curacy of Flamborough and Rectory of Winestead in Yorkshire, was born at Winestead in Holderness on Easter Eve 1621. Three and a half years later his father was elected Master of the Hull Charterhouse, and young Andrew received his early education at the Grammar School in the town, under two graduates of Trinity College, Cambridge, whence he himself matriculated in the University on 14 December 1633, while in his thirteenth year. He remained at Cambridge for the better part of the next eight years, though with at least one significant interval when some Jesuits tempted him to London: his father is said to have found him in a bookseller's shop there and brought him back to the University.

Thereafter his main studies seem to have progressed satisfactorily, and in April 1638 he was elected to a scholarship in the College. A few weeks later his mother, Anne Pease, died, and in the following November his father married the widow Lucy Harris, formerly Alured. In the spring of 1639 Marvell took his Bachelor's degree and was soon on the way to his MA and perhaps an academic career when, in January 1641, his father was drowned crossing the Humber. This critical event seems to have determined – or perhaps freed – him to seek his fortunes in London, and he was no doubt greatly assisted in the scheme by his inheriting some family property in Meldreth, Cambridgeshire.

It is not known at what age Marvell began with serious commitment to compose the poetry that has made him famous in our own time. At Cambridge, though evincing no great desire to shine as an occasional poet, he must have encountered considerable inducements to verse-composition in many walks of University life. The vogue enjoyed by poetry at Cambridge in the 1620s and 1630s has perhaps never been surpassed there: in Marvell's day the colleges abounded in poets of the second and third generations, whose verses were circulated widely in manuscript. At Peterhouse were Crashaw and Beaumont, at St John's Cleveland and Wild, at Magdalen John Saltmarsh, at Emmanuel Clement Paman, at Pembroke William Hammond and Thomas Stanley, at Queen's Nathaniel Whiting, and of course at Trinity itself, where memories of Herbert, Suckling and Randolph were still fresh, the older poet Francis Kynaston and the young Abraham Cowley resided. Moreover, during Marvell's years there much of the best poetry of the early seventeenth century saw print for the first time.

Entry of Marvell's birth in the register of Winestead church, 31 March 1621 (1)

1 Entry of Marvell's birth in the register of Winestead Church, 31 March 1621.

Vicar of Patrington.

'Andrewe the sonne of Andrew Marvell borne Martij ultimo being Easter-even, was baptized Apr: 5to.' This entry is made in the hand of the Reverend Marvell who had been presented to the living of Winestead in Holderness in April 1614 by Sir Christopher Hildyard, the third of that name, whose family had held the advowson for almost two centuries.

The gross annual value of the benefice was £13 19s 6d, of which the Rector had to pay dues totalling £1 19s 6d. The old glebe-house or rectory may have stood on the same site as the elegant one, begun about 1660, which stands a mile or so distant from the church, and there it was that five children were born to the rector and his wife Anne Pease.

The two eldest girls married Master Mariners of Hull while Andrew was still at Cambridge, the second of them becoming the wife of Edmund and mother of William Popple, later a favourite nephew of the poet. Elizabeth, the third child, married Robert More from whose son Fuller had his account (see no. 16) of the Reverend Marvell. A second son, John, was born in 1623 but was buried at Winestead a few days before his father's appointment as Master of the Hull Charterhouse.

BIBLIOGRAPHY: N. J. Miller, *Winestead and its Lords* (Hull, 1932).

2 Winestead Church.

From a print, about 1820.

Winestead Church and the small, scattered community that it serves stand some thirteen miles south-east of Hull, in the low-lying lands of the Holderness peninsula on the north side of the River Humber. At the end of the sixteenth century writers still referred to the district as marshy wasteland, but nevertheless it supported thirty gentlemen's families.

The small Church, which is dedicated to St Germanus, Bishop of Auxerre, one of whose fingers had been brought to Selby Abbey in 1150, was begun about 1170 and consisted simply of a chancel and nave on to which, early in the seventeenth century, Sir Christopher Hildyard built the south transept or chapel that was thereafter used as his family burial-place. In 1619 the Reverend Marvell repaired the chancel, which was ruinous, without altering in any way the fine perpendicular chancel screen. The restored thirteenth-century font, at which young Andrew must have been baptised on 5 April 1621, was brought back to the church, from which it had been removed, in the later nineteenth century.

The church underwent a thorough restoration in 1889, and the living is now joined with that of Patrington.

BIBLIOGRAPHY: George Poulson, *History of Holderness*, vol. 11, p. 466 (London, 1841).

3 Bird's-eye view of Hull from the north-west by Wenceslaus Hollar, about 1640.
Harley MS 2073, f.117.

Hollar, a Bohemian by birth, came to England in 1636 with Thomas Howard, first Earl of Arundel, and was granted the patronage of the royal family. Two years later Daniel Meisner's *Libellus novus politicus emblematicus civitatum* was published, and included a small plate of

Hull engraved by Hollar. In 1639 King Charles sent an officer to survey the defences of the town, and his plan survives in the Public Record Office (MPF 291), but it is not known whether Hollar's larger engraving was connected in any way with this survey. Two editions are known, the later one incorporating in the bottom right-hand corner a small map of south Yorkshire and Lincolnshire, together with a directional compass: these are the only variations, however, and both issues include the view of the town from the river Humber.

The cluster of half-a-dozen buildings with their three walled gardens, occupying an acre and a half of land on the west bank of the river Hull, just outside the North Gate, is God's House of Hull, commonly called the Charterhouse Hospital after the neighbouring Carthusian priory of which it had for a short time been part. During the Reverend Marvell's mastership the institution was in a flourishing condition, the rents at his appointment being advanced to a sum sufficient to maintain the original number of thirteen poor men and thirteen poor women intended by the founder. Young Andrew lived here from his fourth to his thirteenth year, and stayed in the Master's house during the summer vacations until 1641.

Winestead church from a print of 1820 (2)

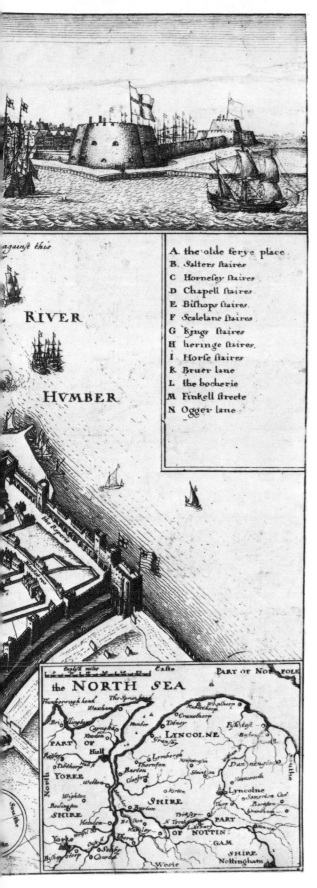

The priory gateway is discernible in Hollar's view between the two rows of buildings of the Charterhouse, while the priory itself is shown standing a few yards to the west. It had been dissolved in 1539 and in the 1620s was the home of the Aldred or Alured family, from whom came the Reverend Marvell's second wife. Both sets of buildings were apparently pulled down by order of Ferdinando, Lord Fairfax, the governor of the garrison at Hull, in September 1643, so that royalist forces might not use them as a siege-point.

BIBLIOGRAPHY: Thomas Sheppard, *The evolution of Kingston-upon-Hull* (Hull, 1911); and John Cook, *The history of God's House of Hull* (Hull, 1882).

4 Holy Trinity Church, Hull.
Photograph by Harry I. Cartlidge.

Holy Trinity, begun at the end of the thirteenth and completed early in the sixteenth century, is in area the largest of English parish churches. In Hollar's view it dominates the centre of the town (see no. 3), having around it a large open churchyard planted with a few trees at the west end. Subsequent restorations have removed various features of the interior that were familiar to Marvell, including the gallery at the west end erected in 1580 for the Grammar School boys when they attended public services. There remains, however, the painted bust of his father's predecessor at the Charterhouse and in the lectureship, Thomas Whincopp, two of whose sons were fellows of Trinity College, Cambridge, during Marvell's time there.

The Reverend Marvell was elected to his two posts simultaneously on 30 September 1624, and his presentation to the Charterhouse was sealed on 2 October. It was the duty of the lecturer or assistant preacher (who should not be confused with the curate or assistant minister) to preach in the church on the afternoons of alternate Sundays and Wednesdays. When the plague raged at Hull in 1637 he distinguished himself by preaching at the funeral of the Mayor.

Birds-eye view of Hull from the north-west by Hollar, about 1640 (3)

The Vicar had introduced a daily service, to win wider acceptance for the Prayer Book among the growing body of puritan opinion, but this was suspended during the plague: a plea by the then Mayor and some aldermen to restore it met with opposition from the puritan curate and was only granted at the intervention of the Archbishop of York whose officials, in 1639, disciplined Marvell also, instructing him to read more of the Prayer Book before his weekly lecture.

BIBLIOGRAPHY: *Victoria History of the County of York, East Riding*, vol. 1 (London, 1969).

5 Old Hull Grammar School, 1978.
Photograph by Harry I. Cartlidge.

The building that in Marvell's time housed the Grammar School and Merchants' Hall was built in 1583–85 at the south-west corner of Holy Trinity Church. It is a simple rectangular building of two storeys lit from the north and south sides by wide windows with brick mullions and transomes, and survives substantially unchanged from what it was in Marvell's day. The cost of its erection was borne jointly by the Corporation, who wanted a schoolhouse, and the Hull Merchants' Company, who needed their own permanent premises; Alderman William Gee made a personal contribution towards the schoolroom.

There is no mention of Marvell among the records relating to the Grammar School but it is almost certain that he was a pupil here between about 1629 and 1633, under two graduates of Trinity College, Cambridge, the Master (1613–May 1632), James Burney and his successor, formerly the Usher (April 1630), Anthony Stevenson. He does not appear to have benefited from the exhibition to an Oxford or Cambridge college that was endowed by the will of Alderman Thomas Ferries in 1631, but on his arrival at Trinity would find Robert Winchester, the first holder of it, already in his third year. Among his closer contemporaries Christopher Fugill went up to Sidney Sussex in July 1633, migrated to Caius in 1636 and took his BA before Marvell.

BIBLIOGRAPHY: John Lawson, *A Town Grammar School through Six Centuries* (London, 1963).

Old Hull Grammar School, 1978 (5)

Alderman Gee's schoolroom, about 1878 (6)

6 Alderman Gee's schoolroom, about 1878.

Drawing by M. T. Satterford from a photograph in Hull City Museums.

Attendance at the Grammar School meant for Marvell a daily walk across the town from the Charterhouse before six in the morning, summer and winter, to take his place among the hundred boys who sat in Alderman Gee's schoolroom. Boys of the Upper School sat in desks grouped around the Master on a raised platform that occupied the top third of the room, while the Usher supervised the rest in the Lower School. On the south side of the school was a large garden where, in May 1632, was built the earliest latrine.

Marvell may have passed his two-hour midday break at the nearby Buttercroft, where the boys played games; the wharves, which gave rise to Parker's charge (in the *Reproof*, 1673, p. 227) of a 'first unhappy Education among Boat-Swains and Cabin-boys, whose Phrases . . . [he] learn'd in [his] Childhood', were probably out of bounds. He certainly spent some of his time at the Artillery Yard, for much later he was to 'remember, though then a child, those blessed days when the youth . . . were trained for [the Hull] militia, and did methought become their arms much better than any soldiers that I have seen there since' (letter to Hull Corporation, 17 Nov. 1660).

At all events, during school hours he received a good grounding in the classical authors, and towards the end of his life recalled that 'this *scanning* was a liberal Art that we learn'd at Grammar School; and to *scan* verses . . . before we did, or were oblidged to understand them' (*Mr. Smirke*), quoting from the *Metamorphoses* of Ovid, the first poet he would have encountered in the Upper School.

BIBLIOGRAPHY: Lawson, *op. cit.*; *VCH York, East Riding, loc. cit.*

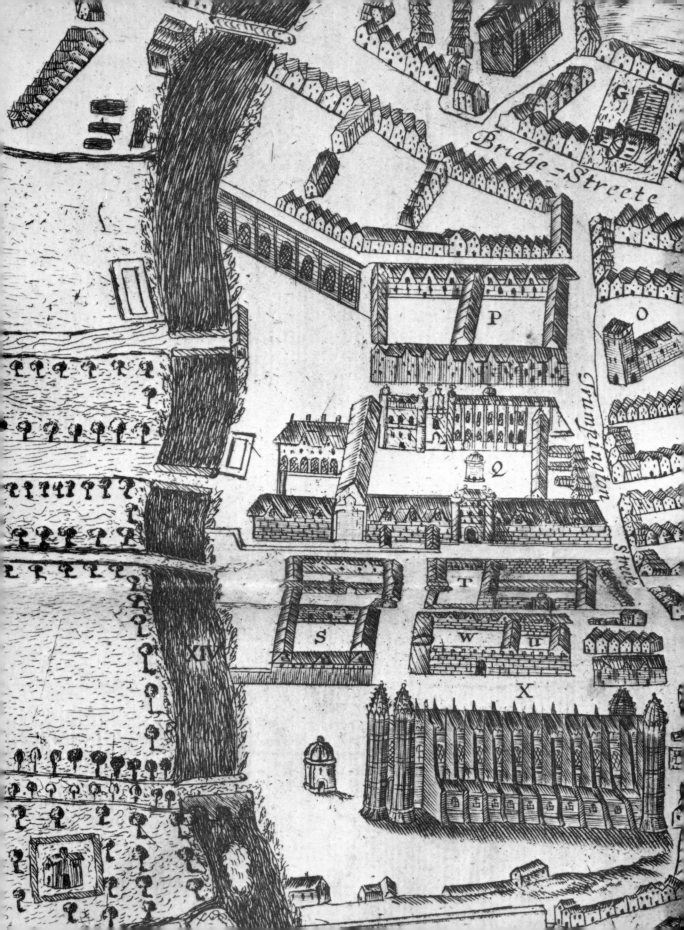

Bridge=Strecte

G

O

P

Q

Trumpington Strecte

XIV

S

T

W

U

X

7 Bird's-eye view of Cambridge in 1634.
483.f.4.

Cantabrigia qualis extitit Anno Domini 1634, the work of an unidentified artist and engraver, was published as the frontispiece to Thomas Fuller's *History of the University of Cambridge* (1655). Though roughly drawn it remains the only view of the University between John Hammond's plan of 1592 and David Loggan's series of designs dating largely from the 1680s, and of these is much the least known. Even during Marvell's time there, Trinity, though the third newest, was the largest of the sixteen colleges, numbering from the Master to the ostler over four hundred persons. The buildings of the medieval King's Hall, later (1546) incorporated into Henry VIII's foundation, had been greatly altered and extended during the Mastership of Thomas Neville (1593–1615), when the First or Great Court, the largest of English collegiate quadrangles, was constructed. The old library occupied the western end of its north range, being separated by King Edward's Tower from the chapel which the Fellows had been stirred to 'beautify' by complaints made to Archbishop Laud, while Marvell was an undergraduate. The placing of the communion table on a raised dais at the east end, as in the new Chapel at Peterhouse, may not, if we believe tradition, have shocked the son of the Puritan Lecturer at Holy Trinity, Hull, as it should have done. The present engraving shows clearly enough the Queen's Gateway in the south, though not the Great Gate in the east range of the Great Court.

In 1634 Neville's Court consisted of two short north and south ranges only, being open to the river: the square shown beside the river, near to the north range, is probably the tennis court that had been built in 1611, when the bridge over the Cam was begun. By the time that Loggan engraved his handsome bird's-eye view from the east the two ranges had been extended to meet the Library begun by Wren in 1677, though otherwise the College remained much as Marvell had known it.

BIBLIOGRAPHY: R. Willis and J. W. Clark, *The Architectural History of the University of Cambridge*, vol. 2, pp. 389–686 (Cambridge, 1886).

8 Praelector's record of Marvell's matriculation at Cambridge, 14 December 1633.
Cambridge University Archives: Matr. 6 (CUR 101.2), f.1254.

When Marvell matriculated from Trinity College he was still only in his thirteenth year, a fact that suggests a certain precocity, coupled perhaps with the fond ambition of his father, who may have secured suitable mentors in the College or outside it for such a young exile from the security of home.

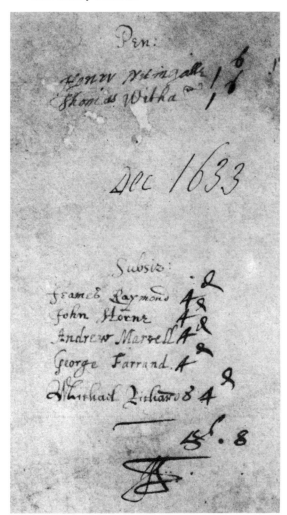

Praelector's record of Marvell's matriculation, 14 December 1633 (8)

The names of students who were to matriculate at a formal ceremony before the Vice-Chancellor were entered on a slip of paper by the Praelector – as the officer who attended to matriculation and graduation was called – of their respective colleges and was submitted to the Registrary of the University who added a note of the fees payable in each case. The Praelector's lists are a primary source of information on admissions to Trinity before College records begin in 1635. Marvell has always been spoken of as a sizar, following the standard reference-work compiled by Rouse Ball and Venn, but the present list shows that, at the time of his matriculation at least, this was not precisely the case. He was in fact entered third in a list of five *Subsiz[atores]* and, as noted by the Registrary James Tabor, whose initials appear at the foot of the entry, paid fourpence to the University on that occasion.

Of the three principal grades of students who were not on the foundation, that is, fellow commoners, pensioners and sizars, the last paid for their board and education in part by the performance of menial tasks for their wealthier contemporaries, receiving an allowance called *liberatura* or livery money of 6s 8d every year, plus a further fourpence a week for food and *reliquias mensae sociorum majorum*. Sixty sizars were thus provided for by the College Statutes, together with an unspecified number of subsizars who, like the former, were admitted after an interview with the Senior Dean and Lector Primarius: though they were granted no allowance for food they were required to pay only a minimal fee for instruction received from the last-named official. Unfortunately the College records are deficient for the earliest years of Marvell's career, though he is known to have been drawing his allowance regularly during the academic year 1636–7.

BIBLIOGRAPHY: *Admissions to Trinity College, Cambridge*, compiled by W. W. Rouse Ball and J. A. Venn, vol. 2 (London, 1913).

9 Συνωδια, sive Musarum Cantabrigiensium Concentus et Congratulatio, 1637.
837.h.16(3).

From time to time the Universities brought out volumes of verse written in celebration of royal events: specially-bound copies were presented to the monarch of these collections in which undergraduates and senior members alike seized the opportunity to show their loyalty and their ingenuity in Greek, Latin or the vernacular. During the 1630s many notable Cambridge poets contributed to collections commemorating the several royal births, and events like the King's return from Scotland in 1633 or his recovery from an illness in 1632; the *Anthologia in Regis Exanthemata* (on the King's pustules) issued on the latter occasion shows how strained the display of loyal affection might become.

The Latin and Greek verses that Marvell wrote for the volume assembled to mark the birth of King Charles's fifth offspring, the Princess Anne, are his earliest known essays in poetry and the first to be published. Though the event took place on 17 March 1637 the authorities began collecting copy well in advance, and Marvell is not the only writer to make no mention of the child's sex. His Greek verses play upon the number of the royal children while his Latin, headed *Ad Regem Carolum Parodia*, are a line-for-line adaptation of Horace's *Odes* 1, 2. A 'parody' in the seventeenth century did not mean an amusing skit but a wholly serious literary exercise in which, as Johnson's *Dictionary* has it, 'the words of an author or his thoughts are taken, and by a slight change adapted to some new purpose'.

10 Letter of the Reverend Andrew Marvell, 6 April 1637.
Lansdowne MS 891, f.118b.

This letter, written from the 'Charthuse' on the day before Good Friday, shows the Reverend Marvell's normal small mixed hand, as well as, in his signature – which resembles that of his son – the bold italic that he used also for entries in the Winestead register.

Letter of
Reverend Andrew Marv
6 April 1637 (

the assumption (in w[hich] the sinews of the arg[ument] lyes) is not unquestionable. It is
said to intend the sacram[ent] onely to those to whome he gave himself, remission of sinnes
&c. I answere 1 the expounding of the gospell, & Christ in it is indefinite, nay universall, in termes,
yet not intended effectually to every individuall here the Arminian stumbles.
2 Christ offers his body blood, remission, & so the ordinances nale & priviledgiate, where
he doth not purpose (much more where he doth not already see) effectuall vocation. as in
Judas.
It is answered that Judas perhaps was away, was not scandalous, was not knowne to Christ
as a minister. But it did not give the elements in particular to Judas

& I thinke the other Evangelists make it plaine that Judas was not gone before y[e] Lords supp[er]
immediately. It is not alwayes taken w[ith]out some latitude. Mat. 29. 29. mar: 28. 2 I suppose that Judas was not notoriously scandalous: as may be gathered probably from mat.
26: 21 &c. 3 Christ as a minister did know long before that Judas was a traitor, a
theife, a devill: for so he had preached him to be formerly. unles it be imagined that
he did not, as a minister, understand himself in those things that he had spoken as a minister. 2 Besides, The divinity did communicate to the humanity though not all, yet,
all convenient knowledge: & I suppose it will be granted to be a thing convenient for ministers
to know the quality of their companies, of those on whome they lay hands, of those to whome
they administer the sacram[ent]. ffurthermore if it were absolutely unlawfull to admit a man
probably a very unworthy person, it should seem that Christ hath layed a stumbling block before the blind, in this his practise to Judas, & leaving the case so dubious. sey p[er]otto.
whether Christ gave the elements in particular to Judas, or no it is not materiall. He gave
to all universally. He interdicted, he excommunicated none. He gave to him mediately. In his
own sight, I suppose, he received it. qui non he did not forbid his receiving. qui non pro-
hibet injuriam, si potest, ille facit. To give there fore was no injury ut videtur.

arg: 2 Much strictnes about the passeover &c.

this argument hath much lesse strength in it. there was required onely ceremoniall
sanctity: that place Exo: 6 21. 2 chron: 23, 19. 35, 15. can be proved no farther.
acknowledged afterward that none were kept away or out for morall impurity
may be noted, that there was not by gods law, among the Iewes, any excommun[ication]
for morall trespasses: that the pharisees did make male mou[...] & it misththe three kinds of excommunication, w[ith]out any divine authority. 3 that the
loci mat: 18. & 1 Cor: 5 used to prove excommunication, in the judgment of very lear-
ned men are thought to look quite another way. 4 that the apost[les] ordinance was to
excommunicate scandalous brethren from civill living, familiar society rather
then Christian assemblyes 1 Cor: 5. 2 Th: 3.   5 that in some Churches lay-magis-
trates do punish all enormities w[ith] sober surtosse for reformation, then our ecclesiasticks
do w[ith] their thunder bolts. & recite these not as my opinions, but as things w[hich] would
be brought under enquiry.
the use w[hich] is layd down in the conclusion of this argum[ent] & suppose, may well receive
satisfaction from what hath been spoken upon the first argument.

3 the marker questioned brings scandall upon religion. and profanes gods holy things &c.
Answ: 1 It may be a scandall taken; not given. 2 the word is not profaned
though delivered to incredulous & dissobedient var[iety]. the marrow & strength of this
doth depend upon the formost reason.

pardon me I beseech you. I write I know not what. I am weary; full of distractions. I preached to day; must preach to morrow. much company about me, many a-
vocations. I have not had two houres to forethink & make up this scrible. Let none
eyes but your own see this abortive. Read, Censure freely, send back my paper y[at]
I may see what I have written. your man calls me off: I must be gone
Pray for me, for a pardon if I erre in this inconsiderate paper. The Lord
guide us into all truth, wisdome, & holines for his glory &c. no more but
Your truly loving friend & brother

Charthuse Apr: 6 1627.

Andr. Marvell

All the letters that are known to survive from the elder Marvell's pen are written to clergymen about some point of theology: here he writes, 'I dare not be so uncharitable as to Censure all those as ignorant or unfaithfull, who administer the sacrament in a maner promiscuously to all Comers . . .' The final paragraph puts us forcibly in mind of Fuller's preacher who 'never broached what he had new brewed':

Sr Pardon me I beseech you: I write I know not what: I am weary; full of distractions. I preache to day; must preach to morrow. Much Company about me, many avocations. I have not had two houres to forethink & make up this scrible. Let none eyes but your own see this abortive. Read, Censure freely, send back my paper that I may see what I have written. Your man Calls me of; I must be gone . . .

We may be fairly certain that the 'Much Company', which probably included his two eldest daughters and their families, did not include Andrew, as expense and distance would have forbidden his return to Hull in any but the long vacation.

11 Marvell's autograph record of his scholarship at Trinity, 13 April 1638.

Trinity College Cambridge: Admission Book of Fellows and Scholars.

Marvell himself entered his new status in the Admission Book after the annual elections in Easter Term, as *Andreas Marvell discipulus*, his being the sixth of thirty-nine such entries on that occasion. The form of the oath to which he had to subscribe is set out in the College Statutes of Elizabeth. By the terms of his scholarship he was entitled to draw an annual *stipendium* of 13s 4d, with a further shilling each week for food, a sum that would be raised by twopence per week on his graduating BA in Lent Term 1639. When, about the time of his graduation, he was promoted to the ranks of the five scholars who benefited from awards made by Lady Bromley he does not seem to have received any further emoluments, but during the next academic year (1639–40) continued to draw his stipend each quarter.

It is possible to flesh out a little these bare bones by adding a few details about the academic regimen that obtained during this period at Trinity: it was, in theory at least, both strenuous and authoritarian. At five in the morning the students rose, sat in Chapel and heard one of the Fellows 'commonplace it' for over an hour, then, after breakfast, attended tutorials and college lectures. At Trinity the latter were delivered by special 'Lectors' who taught their respective subjects for an hour and a half each day. Dinner at twelve was followed by lectures in the public schools of the University, which done the students had some free time before evening chapel at six and supper at seven, and again before the gates of the College closed at nine in winter and ten in summer.

BIBLIOGRAPHY: *Documents relating to the University and Colleges of Cambridge*, vol. 3, pp. 365–477 (London, 1852); and H. F. Fletcher, *The Intellectual Development of John Milton*, vol. 2, *passim* (Urbana, 1961).

12 Copy of the record of Marvell's scholarship, taken in 1773.

Add. MS 5846, f.133b.

This copy of awards and elections made in Trinity College during the sixteenth and seventeenth centuries was taken from a volume of collections compiled by Dr Charles Mason, FRS (d.1771) by the Cambridge antiquary William Cole (1714–82) who remarked that Mason's '*Method & Manner* of *arranging* his *Names & Dates* are *confused* to an *unaccountable Degree*'. For the mid-seventeenth century Mason's authority was the Admission Book of Fellows and Scholars (see no. 11), but in the case of the 1638 elections to scholarships he added extra information from an unknown source.

The first eight entries in this list run as follows:

Sam. Collins	cho. 40
Gul. Robson	Cond. 40. 42
Geor. Meade	cho. 40–42
Gul. Barnard	chor. 40–sc. 42
Hen. Aiscough	40. 42
Andr. Marvell	cho. 40–42
Edw. Wakefield	40
Edw. Waterhouse	cho. 42

Disscipuli iurati et admissi 1638. Aprilis 13°.

Samuel Collins iuratus et admissus.

Gulielmus Robson disscipulus iuratus et admissus
Georgius Meade juratus et admissus.
Gulielmus Barnard disscipulus iuratus et admissus
Henricus Aiscongh disscipulus juratus et admissus
Andreas Marvell disscipulus juratus et admissus
Edvardus Wakefeild. Disscipulus et admissus
Edvardus Waterhouse disscipulus iuratus et admissus.

Marvell's entry in Trinity College Admission Book of Scholars, 13 April 1638 (11)

The abbreviation 'cho.' or 'chor.' must stand for *chorista* or chorister, of whom ten – *decem pueri Symphoniaci qui Choristae nominentur* – were provided for in the College Statutes; while 'Cond.' means the Conduct, who was appointed to read prayers in the Chapel.

Tempting as it may be to believe that the future poet of *Musicks Empire*, *The Fair Singer* and other lyrics probably written to be set to music took an active part in the musical life of his College, we must nevertheless maintain some reservations about the matter because of the dates quoted. Marvell is unlikely to have retained any place in the College books as late as the end of March 1641/2.

13 Marvell's autograph subscription for his Bachelor's degree, February 1639.

Cambridge University Archives: Subscriptiones II, f.9.

In 1613, at the command of King James, the Senate had passed a Grace by which all holders of superior degrees must subscribe to the 'Three Articles of Religion' that involved recognition of the royal supremacy in ecclesiastical and temporal matters, together with unqualified acceptance of the Book of Common Prayer and the Thirty-Nine Articles. By 1616 this requirement had been extended also to candidates for inferior degrees: the whole business was abolished by Parliament in 1640.

Subscriptiones Questionistarum
Anno Dm 1638
Dre. Brownrigg Procam
Herbertus Thorndike   Thorndike
                                        Procuratoribus.
Richardus Bryan.   Briant

Coll. Regal.

We whose names are heere underwritten doe willingly and
ex animo subscribe to the three articles before mentioned
and to all things in them conteyned.

                              Edward Wilkinson
        Laurentius Lister   John Remington
Fellows Thomas Almon   Manabel Ryme
        Johannes Byng

Coll: Trinitatis.

Wee whose names are hereunder written, Doe
willinglie & ex animo Subscribe to the three articles
aboue mentioned & to all things in them contayned.

Thomas Petter   Thomas Wray
Humfrey Babington
Henry Aislough   Robert North   Tho. Turnor
William Smith   Richard Hull   Timothy Wolf ...
Marmaduke James   Timothy Donison   Francis Squire
William Robson   John Nicholas   Thomas Chadwell
Thomas Wright   Peter Drinkwater   William Trevis
Jonathan ffoster   Samuel Collins
Andrew Warner   George Meade   Edward Hawa...
No Supp: John ffauleons William Barnard
Charles Wheeler   Andrew Marvell
Edward Campian   Edward Wakefeild
William Moore   Gerard Skrymsher
No Supp: William Cornwall Timothy Wood
Thomas Griffin   Richard Burton
Michaell Marshall   John Duckett
Andrew Johnson   Richard Culvervell
Thomas Harris   John Dowie
Edward Waterhouse   HENRY Gosnold

Of the forty-four members of Trinity who subscribed to the articles in the presence of the Registrary before 27 February 1639 only forty-two actually supplicated for the degree in that term. Marvell's name occurs in twenty-ninth place among the former and thirty-third place among the latter, though the order itself is probably of no consequence.

Marvell's subscription is the only surviving autograph record of the events connected with his Bachelor's degree, for which he supplicated after having been on the register of the University for seventeen terms, that is, five more than was required by the Statutes. Since first degrees were almost always awarded in the Lent Term, the Easter Term of four years previously was normally taken as the first reckonable one, though all those who matriculated with Marvell in December 1633 took their BAs in Lent 1637, the eleventh only of their residence in Cambridge.

It is possible that early in 1637 and again in 1638 the authorities at Trinity regarded Marvell as too little advanced in his studies or too young, at an age when most students were only just matriculating, to stand as questionist in the Schools. His was certainly not the only case in which a degree was taken after five, instead of four years. Yet it may be that this delay was owing to another reason, such as a period of illness or a temporary absence from the University of another sort. Cooke's story, presumably derived from family tradition, of his seduction away from Cambridge by Jesuits (see no. 14) springs to mind.

14 Letter from the Reverend John Norton to the Reverend Marvell, about January 1640.
Hull City Archives: L.247.

Until Grosart's discovery of this unsigned and undated letter, lacking also an address, no independent evidence was known to exist for an episode relating to Marvell's life at Cambridge that Thomas Cooke may have had from the family:

He had not been long there, before his Studys were interrupted by this remarkable Accident. Some *Jesuits*, with whom he was then conversant, seeing in him a Genius beyond his Years, thought of Nothing less than gaining a Proselyte. And doubtless their Hopes extended farther. They knew, if that Point was once obtained, he might in Time be a great Instrument towards carrying on their Cause. They used all the Arguments they could to seduce him away, which at last they did. After some Months his Father found him in a *Bookseller*'s Shop in *London*, and prevailed with him to return to the College.

Margoliouth identified the writer of the letter as the Vicar of Welton, a village ten miles west of Hull, and from internal references dated it with high probability to January 1640. Norton, relating the seduction of his son, then at Catherine Hall, by Jesuits, writes: 'I perceive by Mr Breercliffe some such prank used towards your sonne: I desire to know what you did therin . . .'

From the proximity of Welton to Hull, Margoliouth argued that Norton's mentioning the younger Marvell's temporary conversion implies that it was a recent event, but the letter need not bear this interpretation. Nothing is known of Marvell's undergraduate career, whereas in 1639 he took his BA degree – subscribing, amongst other things, to the Thirty Nine Articles – and was elected to a scholarship in April: from Michaelmas 1639 to 1640 he received his *stipendium* regularly every quarter. His absence for 'some Months' in London during the summer might have thrown his scholarship into jeopardy.

BIBLIOGRAPHY: *Modern Language Review*, XVII (1922), pp. 353–5.

Marvell's name in Trinity College Conclusion Book, 24 September 1641 (15)

15 Marvell forfeits his place in Trinity College, 24 September 1641.

Trinity College, Cambridge: Conclusion Book.

Towards the end of the Long Vacation of 1641 the following entry was made in the Trinity Conclusion Book: 'It is agreed by the Master and 8 Seniors that Mr Carter, and D^s Wakefeild^s, D^s Marvell, D^s Waterhouse, and D^s Maye, in regard that some of them are reported to be maryed and the others looke not after their dayes nor Acts, shall receave no more benefitt of the College, and shalbe out of their places unles they shew just cause to the College for the Contrary in 3 months'.

By this period the requirements for intending Masters of Arts were minimal: residence for the

full nine terms had been abandoned in 1608 and consequently it is likely that only a very few essential 'dayes' and 'Acts', that is attendances at public exercises in the Schools, had to be kept. It looks therefore as if Marvell's transgression was both flagrant and of some duration: most probably he had gone down shortly after his father's death in January of this year. Three of the other offenders mentioned had been elected to scholarships with Marvell in 1638 and none of them took his Master's degree. Edward Wakefield and Edward Waterhouse may have been Yorkshireman, Theophilus May seems to have taken up medicine, dying abroad by 1650, while 'Mr Carter' is probably the Thomas Carter who had taken his MA in the previous July, having been Master of Highgate School since at least 1639. If he had kept his name on the college books intending to take a higher degree he might have forfeited his place by marriage.

16 Fuller's account of the Reverend Andrew Marvell, 1662.
613.1.8.

Thomas Fuller (1608–61), a Cambridge man and moderate divine who achieved fame as a historical writer, began compiling his *Worthies of England* at some time during the Civil War: it was published after his death by his son. For the erroneous statement that the Reverend Marvell was a Master of Arts of Trinity College (instead of Emmanuel) Fuller gives as his authority the Reverend Marvell's son-in-law – or more probably his grandson, Thomas More, a Fellow of Magdalene – but the remainder of his account is probably accurate enough.

He afterwards became Minister in *Hull*, where for his life time he was well beloved. Most *facetious* in his *discourse*, yet *grave* in his *carriage*, a most excellent preacher, who like a good husband never *broached* what he had new *brewed*, but preached what he had pre-studied some competent time before. Insomuch that he was wont to say, that he would crosse the common proverb, which called *Saturday the working day, and Munday the holy day of preachers.* It happened that *Anno Dom.* 1640. *Jan.* 23. crossing *Humber* in a *Barrow-boat*, the same was *sand-warpt*, and he [With Mrs. *Skinner* (daughter to Sir *Ed. Coke*) a very religious Gentlewoman] drowned therein, by the *carelessness* (not to say *drunkenness*) of the boat-men, to the great grief of all good men. His excellent comment upon Saint *Peter*, is daily desired and expected, if the *envy* and *covetousness* of private persons for their *own use*, deprive not the publick of the benefit thereof.

Abraham de la Pryme, who calls Marvell 'a Verry Learned, Ingenious & Florid Man' (Lansdowne MS 890, f.94b), concurs in this description of his death, though with some embellishment.

Trinity College Great Court, showing the conduit, Chapel (left) and Great Gate

London and the Continent

Oh Thou, that dear and happy Isle
The Garden of the World ere while,
Thou *Paradise* of four Seas,
Which *Heaven* planted us to please,
But, to exclude the World, did guard
With watry if not flaming Sword;
What luckless Apple did we tast,
To make us Mortal, and Thee Wast.
Upon Appleton House, st. XLI

ARVELL left Cambridge, perhaps in the summer of 1641, and by the following February was lodging in Cowcross, near St John Street in Clerkenwell, an easy walk away from the Inns of Court where in the same month he may have witnessed the transfer of land between two distinguished Yorkshiremen. We do not know whether he was brought in by one of the main parties or by another witness, but in either case we may suspect that he was a student at one of the Inns.

At some time possibly as early as the summer of 1642, but at all events not later than autumn 1643, Marvell set out for the continent, spending the next four years in Holland, France, Italy and Spain: he may therefore have been absent from England during the whole period of the First Civil War. The merest traces of his experiences abroad survive in his poetry and in his later prose works: in 'Fleckno, *an English Priest at* Rome' he recounts, with a wealth of witty hyperbole, an incident that probably took place early in 1646. It has generally been assumed that he travelled as tutor-companion to a young man of rank or wealth, but not impossibly he made the tour on his own small patrimony: in November 1647, seemingly not long after his return, he sold a second portion of some property inherited from his grandfather.

The record of the sale describes him as of Hull, but if he spent some time there after his return he soon moved to the capital again, for by 1648 or 1649 he was moving in London literary circles. His contributing to Lovelace's *Lucasta* and to the volume of elegies on Lord Hastings' death tells us a little about the company that he was keeping at this period, though the assumption of royalist sympathies is a rather debatable matter. These, if they existed in any serious sense, gave way by the summer of 1650 to, at the least, a personal admiration of Cromwell. As regards a career Marvell may have resumed his connection with the Inns of Court, while in poetical terms the assurance of manner and control of the verse medium shown in the pieces from 'Fleckno' to the 'Horatian *Ode*' argues a lengthy apprenticeship to the muse.

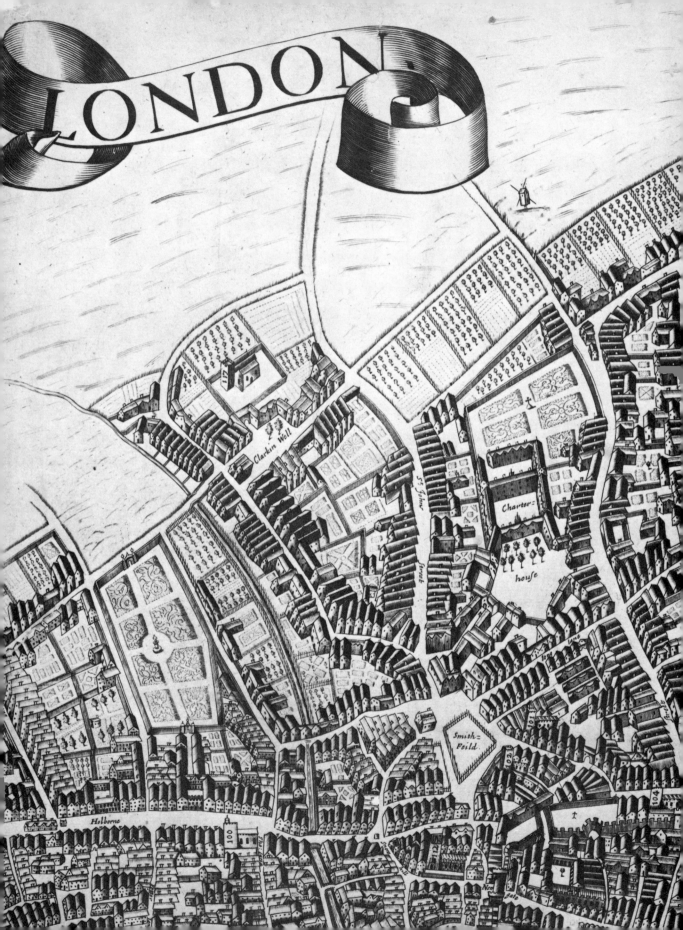

LONDON

Clarkin Well

St John streat

Charter house

Smith Feild

long lane

Holborne

17 Marvell subscribes to the Protestation in Clerkenwell, 17 February 1642.

House of Lords Record Office:
Protestation Returns.

On 3 May 1641 the Commons ordered each of its members to subscribe to an undertaking that ran as follows. 'I *A.B.* do . . . promise, vow, and protest, to maintain and defend . . . the true, reformed Protestant Religion . . . according to the Duty of my Allegiance to his Majesty's Royal Person, Honour, and Estate; as also the Power and Privilege of Parliament, the lawful Rights and Liberties of the Subjects . . .' In January 1642 this 'Protestation', which had been printed, was extended to the country at large and the returns came in with surprising rapidity.

Marvell's name is included in the 'Return of Robert List (Constable) on the North Syde of Cowcrosse . . . of the names of the several persons which dwell within the said Liberty . . .' who had signed the Protestation. Cowcross, which runs from Farringdon Road to St John Street in Clerkenwell, is clearly shown in the map-view of about 1590 that is ascribed to Ralph Agas and, somewhat crudely, in Faithorne's engraving of 1658 (see no. 56). The area had been fashionable at a slightly earlier period than that of the Civil War, and well-to-do families still had town houses there by the Restoration. It bordered on the quarter known commonly as 'St. Jones' whence Marvell addressed a letter to Hull Corporation on 19 May 1663.

BIBLIOGRAPHY: Pauline Burdon, 'Marvell after Cambridge', *British Library Journal*, vol. IV, no. 1 (spring 1978), forthcoming; *Commons Journals*, II, 132; Historical Manuscripts Commission, 5th Report, 1876, p. 3.

18 Marvell witnesses a deed of mortgage, 21 February 1642.

Sotheron-Estcourt Papers (Humberside County Record Office) DDSE(2) 16/146.

This is the third in a series of similar deeds (DDSE (2) 16/62 A & B and 16/146), dated 8, 10 and 21 February respectively, that record the transfer of land and other property in Darrington, Yorkshire, by Sir William Savile of

Witnesses to the Savile deed of 21 February 1642 (18)

Thornhill to Thomas, Viscount Savile of Pontefract. Together with the Protestation return (see no. 17), also discovered by Mrs Burdon, they reveal for the first time Marvell's whereabouts immediately after he left Cambridge.

The identity of two other witnesses to the deed of 21 February, namely Robert Lewys, a barrister of Gray's Inn who had witnessed several Savile deeds in the past, and William Rosse, attorney of Furnivall's Inn, makes it fairly likely that the deeds were drawn up at the Inns of Court. Lewys, Rosse and Marvell signed all three deeds, while the name of William Steed, possibly a student at the Middle Temple or a Yorkshireman from the Leeds area is found only on the two latest, and that of the unknown Thomas Graunt only on the last.

It is possible that Marvell, who was living at this time in Cowcross, not far east of the Inns of Court, may have enrolled as a student of law, perhaps in one of the smaller Societies whose records have not survived. On the other hand, as one of the Saviles is known from an undated but apparently somewhat later source to have had a house in 'St Jones', as that area of Clerkenwell was popularly called, it may be that Marvell worked for him in some capacity, or at least was sufficiently acquainted with the family to make himself available when the lawyers called to complete the transaction.

BIBLIOGRAPHY: Pauline Burdon, *loc. cit.*

19 'Fleckno, *an English Priest at* Rome', about March 1646.

G.2449(3).

Oblig'd by frequent visits of this man,
Whom as Priest, Poet, and Musician,
I for some branch of *Melchizedeck* took,
(Though he derives himself from *my Lord Brooke*)
I sought his Lodging; which is at the Sign
Of the sad *Pelican*; Subject divine
For Poetry: There three Stair-Cases high,
Which signifies his triple property,
I found at last a Chamber, as 'twas said,
But seem'd a Coffin set on the Stairs head.

Richard Flecknoe, the unfortunate target of Marvell's earliest surviving satire as well as of Dryden's *MacFlecknoe* (1682), was in Rome between 1645 and 1647. When Marvell, 'Oblig'd by frequent visits', called on him, apparently in Lent 1646, he was living in the meanest of lodgings at the Pelican Inn: his famished condition, his subservience to a rich young coxcomb and his readiness to recite reams of his own bad verse prompted this amusing if hyperbolical poem, that derives from Horace by way of Donne. Such a virtuoso performance presupposes a sympathetic audience, so that most probably Marvell wrote it to divert his companions at the time, or possibly as a *pièce de salon* to amuse the members of a London literary circle on his return. At all events, Flecknoe, whose social snobbery is well known, could have had two reasons for cultivating the young traveller: Marvell was evidently living in more affluent circumstances, and may have had the reputation of a poet.

During his four years abroad, as we learn from Milton, Marvell visited Holland, France, Italy and Spain, presumably in that order, and 'to very good purpose, as I beleeve, & the gaining of those 4 languages'. If Marvell had benefited sufficiently from his travels for it to appear in an interview with the more experienced man we may wonder why, apart from the present satire, they left no more evident mark upon his poetry than a few oblique references in *Upon Appleton House* (1650–2) and 'The Character of Holland' (1653). In the former he recalls his sojourn in Spain with a remark about the bull-ring in Madrid and mentions of the 'Bel Retiro' and Aranjuez, both of which are close to the capital. Later, in the letter to a friend in Persia (1671), he speaks of his 'Fencing-master in *Spain*' in such a way as to imply not only a fairly prolonged stay there but also a rather gentlemanly mode of living.

BIBLIOGRAPHY: Pauline Burdon, 'Andrew Marvell and Richard Flecknoe in Rome', *Notes and Queries*, January 1972, pp.16–18.

20 Marvell sells property in Meldreth, 12 November 1647.

Humberside County Libraries: Hull Central Library.

Together with the Lovelace and Hastings poems these two documents, here exhibited for the first time, supply the only certain information that we have so far acquired about Marvell's movements after his return from the continent, as well as giving valuable details about his private means. It now appears that his 'foure yeares' abroad must have fallen at some time between February 1642 and November 1647, and we may guess that he left England soon after the outbreak of the First Civil War, returning after its close.

On his return, when described as 'of Kingstone super Hull Gentleman', he disposed of some property in Meldreth, Cambridgeshire, that must have descended to him from his grandfather, who died at Hull in 1628, having left his native county rather than pay an enforced loan to the King. The terms of the sale as recorded in the principal (counterpart) deed, negotiated with a certain John Stacey of Orwell who may have been a relation of Marvell's contemporary of the same name at Trinity, show that the property consisted of a 'Messuage or Tenement with a Croft to the same adioyninge And one Close of land conteyninge by Estimation three acres and a halfe bee it more or lesse'. Moreover it emerges also that Marvell had previously sold two adjacent plots of land to Stacey, almost certainly before leaving for the continent.

The second and smaller deed is a bond with defeasance, and on the verso of the principal deed it is noted that Marvell himself was present in Meldreth to deliver seisin on 23 December. The

Marvell's signature to the Meldreth deed of 12 November 1647 (20)

signatures on the present deeds are barely recognisable as those of the young man who entered his name in the Admission Book of Scholars in 1638 (see no.11) or who witnessed the Savile transaction in 1642 (no.18). The only real distinguishing feature that they share is the twist given, indifferently and not invariably, to the first stroke of the 'w' or 'v'.

BIBLIOGRAPHY: W. H. Kelliher, 'Some Notes on Andrew Marvell', *British Library Journal*, vol. IV, no. 2 (autumn 1978), forthcoming.

21 Map of Meldreth in Cambridgeshire, 1886.
Map Library: Ordnance Survey 1: 2,500

The house and land that Marvell had inherited from his grandfather lay, as defined in the deeds of 1647, between the north–south highway called 'the south end streete' and the brook that runs roughly parallel to it on the east, called 'Fulbrooke'. These are clearly indicated in the 25-inch Ordnance Survey of 1886, along with the acreage of lands lying between field boundaries that had been registered mainly by the enclosure of 1820, but of which some at least followed much older divisions. It may not be wholly coincidence, therefore, that the house known formerly as 'The Marvells', but by 1886 as 'Meldreth Court', stands within this strip of land between the road and the brook.

It is not known on what authority Dr W. M. Palmer, the Cambridgeshire antiquary (quoted in Additional MS 39814, f. 271b) stated that the house took its name from a branch of the Mar-vells that remained in Meldreth in the later seventeenth century.

BIBLIOGRAPHY: W. M. Palmer, *The Neighbourhood of Melbourn & Meldreth* (repr. from the *Cambridge Chronicle*, July 1923).

22 Portrait of Thomas Stanley: copy, late eighteenth or early nineteenth century.
G.11435 (1).

The British Library copy of Stanley's *Poems*, 1651, incorporates a portrait admirably executed during the later eighteenth or early nineteenth century in monochrome watercolour, probably from an engraving of the portrait formerly ascribed to Lely but more recently to Gerard Soest; this dates from about 1660 and is now in the National Portrait Gallery.

Stanley, who was born four years after Marvell and died four months before him, was tutored privately by the classical scholar William Fairfax, going up to Pembroke College, Cambridge, in 1639 at the desire of his uncle, the poet William Hammond, whom he joined there. On the outbreak of civil war he went to France and travelled there for some years, returning to study at the Middle Temple by 1646, when he contributed commendatory poems to John Hall's *Essays*, Shirley's *Poems* and Suckling's *Fragmenta Aurea*. At the same time he assembled a manuscript collection of his own poems, now in Cambridge University Library, from which they were prepared for private publication in the following year. His circle of friends

Miniature portrait of Thomas Stanley,
inserted in his *Poems*, 1651 (22)

Friends', includes, in pieces like 'Celia *sleeping
or singing*' and *The Return* – occuring in a single
opening of the text – and in the translation of
Time Recover'd, rhymes and images that may
recall or else anticipate *To his Coy Mistress*.

More significantly perhaps, Stanley's ren-
dering of the sixteenth poem from Johannes
Secundus's *Basia* employs the metre that Marvell used for the 'Horatian *Ode*':

Thou then *Latona's* Star more bright,
Fairer then *Venus* golden Light,
    A hundred Kisses pay;
    Many as *Lesbia*
Gave and receiv'd from her glad Lover;
As are the Graces round thee hover,
    Or Cupids that do skip
    About thy Cheek, and Lip . . .

This translation was first published in the 1651
Poems: a version written in a rather different
metre survives in Cambridge University Library MS Add. 7514, a fair copy of his poems that
Stanley had copied about 1646. One wonders
whether the new version was inspired by a sight
of the ode that Marvell composed in the summer
of 1650.

BIBLIOGRAPHY: *The Poems and Translations of
Thomas Stanley*, ed. G. M. Crump (Oxford, 1962).

at the Temple included the above-mentioned
poets, together with his 'cousin' Edward Sher-
burne, Herrick and Lovelace. After the King's
execution he retired to Hertfordshire and there
busied himself in revising and augmenting his
poems for the edition that Moseley published in
1651.

23 Thomas Stanley, *Poems and Translations,* 1647.
C.71.bb.7.

Despite the fact that their careers seem to have
overlapped at several points Stanley and Marvell have never attracted much attention as
possible acquaintances. This is the more curious
since Stanley's latest editor repeatedly calls attention to the way that his verse in matter and
manner finds echoes in Marvell's own. Though
a less original and adaptable artist than Marvell,
he was master of the same literatures, translating excellently from the classical poets and,
among the moderns, from Guarini, Marino,
Gongora, Vega, De Viau, Theophile, St Amant
and others. The *Poems and Translations* of 1647,
which was 'Printed for the Author, and his

24 George, second Duke of Buckingham and Lord Francis Villiers by Jan Baptist Gaspers, after Van Dyck.
B.M. Department of Prints and Drawings:
1888–12–21–5.

Francis Villiers, the third but second surviving
son of the first Duke of Buckingham, was born
on 2 April 1629, seven months after the murder
of his father. King Charles brought him up with
his own children: in March 1642 he received an
MA from Trinity College, Cambridge, and during 1646 and 1647 travelled in France and Italy.
Clarendon described him as 'of rare beauty and
comeliness of person'. In June 1648 his elder
brother George and he joined the Earl of Holland in a plot to relieve Colchester, but their
troop having failed on 7 July to take Reigate
Castle they fell back on Kingston:

Drawing of the Villiers brothers by Gaspe[rs]
from a portrait after Van Dyck (2

On the same day the brothers were declared traitors and their lands were sequestrated: part was granted in November 1650 (see B.L. Add. Charter 1800) to Lord Fairfax – a fine irony if Mary Fairfax's tutor were really the author of the Villiers elegy. George managed to slip away to France, and Francis was subsequently buried in Westminster Abbey.

This drawing in red chalk, thought to be of the two Villiers brothers, was taken from an oil-painting executed in the style of Van Dyck (National Gallery cat. no. 3605) that is inscribed 'Lord John and Lord Bernard Stuart'.

BIBLIOGRAPHY: S. R. Gardiner, *History of the Great Civil War*, vol. IV, pp. 160–1 (London, 1893); E. Croft-Murray and P. Hulton, *Catalogue of British Drawings*, p. 326 and pl. 129 (London, 1960).

25 'An Elegy upon the Death of my Lord *Francis Villiers*', after 7 July 1648.
Worcester College, Oxford.

The apparently unique surviving quarto of this elegy bears a manuscript attribution to Marvell by George Clarke (1661–1736), the politician and virtuoso who left a splendid collection of books, manuscripts and drawings to Worcester College. C. H. Wilkinson, who discovered the attribution, has amply illustrated Clarke's literary and antiquarian tastes, and the accuracy of his attributions of contemporary pamphlets. The present elegy seems to hint at some acquaintance with Villiers, his private affairs and the manner of his death. It is possible that Marvell met him during his own last months at Trinity – though he was presumably not present at the degree ceremony in March 1642 – or that they became acquainted on the continent. Nevertheless, grave doubts may be felt about his supposed authorship of this piece.

Despite the writer's technical competence – not always faultless, however – his command of classical myth and literary reference and his familiarity with contemporary poetic conventions, the stumbling-block to Marvell's authorship lies not so much in the verses that look forward to the death of 'heavy Cromwell'

To his Noble Friend Mr. *Richard Lovelace*, upon his POEMS.

SIR,

OVr times are much degenerate from those (chose,
Which your sweet Muse which your fair Fortune
And as complexions alter with the Climes,
Our wits have drawne th'infection of our times.
That candid Age no other way could tell
To be ingenious, but by speaking well.
Who best could prayse, had then the greatest prayse,
Twas more esteem'd to give, then weare the Bayes:
Modest ambition studi'd only then,
To honour not her selfe, but worthy men.
These vertues now are banisht out of Towne,
Our Civill Wars have lost the Civicke crowne.
He highest builds, who with most Art destroys,
And against others Fame his owne employs.
I see the envious Caterpillar sit
On the faire blossome of each growing wit.
    The Ayre's already tainted with the swarms
Of Insects which against you rise in arms.
Word-peckers, Paper-rats, Book-scorpions,
Of wit corrupted, the unfashion'd Sons.
The barbed Censurers begin to looke
Like the grim consistory on thy Booke;

And

Marvell's commendatory verses from *Lucasta*, 1649 (26)

Lord Francis Villiers . . . had thrown himself into the midst of the rear guard, which bore the brunt of the attack. His horse having been killed under him he continued to defend himself vigorously with his back against an elm tree which rose from a hedge, till one of Livesey's soldiers, slipping to the other side of the hedge, dashed his steel cap off his head and slew him from behind.

and the 'long-deceived Fairfax', which contrast so flagrantly with his admiration for these men in 1650, as in the concluding lines which are the utterance of a bigoted royalist, himself probably under arms, who savagely (and accurately) promises a renewal of civil war.

Three other elegies that were published on this sad event are preserved among the Thomason Tracts, one of them, a broadside, being dated by the bookseller as early as 4 August. Most of these verse-tributes are addressed, directly or indirectly, not to Villiers' mother who had remarried and was living in Ireland, but to his sister the beautiful Duchess of Richmond, whom Van Dyck had portrayed as St Agnes and whose husband was Keeper of Richmond Park, which overlooks Kingston (cf. ll. 7, 8 of the Worcester College elegy).

26 'To his Noble Friend Mr. *Richard Lovelace*, upon his Poems', 1649.
238. b.52.

Lucasta was licensed on 4 February 1648 but not entered in the Stationers' Registers until 14 May 1649, between which dates the author was imprisoned for nine months in London. Marvell's reference to the 'barbed Censurers' has been taken to imply that his commendatory verses were composed before the licence was granted, but Kent's 'first petition' suggests a date after 2 May 1648. A disturbance in the order of the preliminary matter in the present copy, which makes Marvell's the first of the commendatory poems, has been interpreted by Lovelace's editor as a deliberate act of deference; it is not easy to see why this should be so, since others probably were closer friends and better-known poets.

The names of the other contributors confirm that Marvell was in royalist company, and possibly moving in Inns of Court circles, for they include three Cambridge contemporaries, three men who had been or still were at Gray's Inn, John Harmar, under-Master at Westminster, future Professor of Greek at Oxford, and a friend of Herrick, and John Hall who, also from Gray's Inn, kept up a friendship with the circle

And on each line cast a reforming eye,
Severer then the yong Presbytery.
Till when in vaine they have thee all perus'd,
You shall for being faultlesse be accus'd.
Some reading your Lucasta, will alledge
You wrong'd in her the Houses Priviledge.
Some that you under sequestration are,
Because you write when going to the Warre,
And one the Book prohibits, because Kent
Their first Petition by the Authour sent.
  But when the beauteous Ladies came to know
That their deare Lovelace was endanger'd so:
Lovelace that thaw'd the most congealed brest,
He who lov'd best. and them defended best.
Whose hand so rudely grasps the steely brand,
Whose hand so gently melts the Ladies hand.
They all in mutiny though yet undrest
Sally'd, and would in his defence contest.
And one the loveliest that was yet e're seen,
Thinking that I too of the rout had been.
Mine eyes invaded with a female spight,
(She knew what pain't would be to lose that sight.
O no, mistake not, I reply'd, for I
In your defence, or in his cause would dy.
But he secure of glory and of time
Above their envy, or mine aid doth clime.
Him, valianst men, and fairest Nymphs approve,
His Booke in them finds Judgement, with you Lov

Andr. Marvell.

of Thomas Stanley. Marvell, Hall and Harmar all obtained posts under the Parliament, or in Parliamentary circles, in the year after *Lucasta* was published, and all three were contributors to *Lachrymae Musarum* (see no. 28).

BIBLIOGRAPHY: *Poems of Richard Lovelace*, ed. by C. H. Wilkinson (Oxford, 1930); Kelliher, *loc. cit.*

Engraved portrait
of Richard Lovelace
by Hollar, 1659 (27)

27 Engraved portrait of Lovelace by Hollar, about 1659.

B. M. Department of Prints and Drawings:
Parthey 1692.

A second volume of Lovelace's poems, entitled
'*Lucasta. Posthume Poems . . .*' appeared two
years after his death under the auspices of his
younger brother, Dudley Posthumous Lovelace, assisted by Eldred Revett. It was entered
in the Stationers' Register on 14 November
1659. The preliminary matter is contained in
four leaves, of which the first two carry on their
rectos the title-page and the dedication by Dudley Lovelace, while the other two have either an
engraved portrait of the author by Faithorne or
Hollar, each to be found in any one of three
states, with the remaining leaf blank, or both
engravings together and no blank. The first state
of the Hollar print is, as shown here, undated; a
second was produced in 1660 and a third in
1662. Lovelace's portrait was evidently in demand at the Restoration.

Lovelace had been incorporated MA at
Cambridge in October 1637, and may have
stayed there for some months before moving to
London and the Court. The next few years were
spent as a soldier and a country gentleman, but
after his part in presenting the Kentish Petition
in April 1642 – an event mentioned in Marvell's
commendatory verses (ll. 31, 32) – he was
imprisoned in London, being released in June.
According to C. H. Wilkinson he 'spent a part
and probably the greater part of the years
1643–6 in Holland and France', at some time
after the fall of Dunkirk in October 1646 returned home, and is met with in London in the
following October. It is not known whether
Marvell encountered him first at Cambridge,
or during his four years abroad, or after his
return to England in 1647, but neither his
prefatory verses to *Lucasta* nor internal resem-
blances within their poetry suggest too great
an influence from the elder's work. Despite
seeming points of comparison between

'Amyntor's Grove' and *The Gallery*, 'Aramantha' and *Upon Appleton House*, only one definite reminiscence has been traced, (cf. the 'Dialogue' between Lucasta and Alexis, ll.15,16 and *The unfortunate Lover* ll. 57, 58).

BIBLIOGRAPHY: L. N. Wall, 'Some notes on Marvell's sources', *Notes and Queries*, April 1957, pp. 170–3.

28 **'Lachrymae Musarum; The Tears of the Muses: Exprest in Elegies; written by divers persons of Nobility and Worth, upon the death of the most hopefull Henry Lord Hastings . . .', 1649.**
C.117.b.32.

Henry, Lord Hastings, only son of Ferdinando, twenty-third Earl of Huntingdon, died in his twentieth year of smallpox, on 24 June 1649, the eve of his marriage to a daughter of Sir Theodore Mayerne, the King's physician. His funeral took place on 4 July, the procession passing from Covent Garden to St John Street, Clerkenwell. The dramatist Richard Brome edited a volume of elegies on the deceased, of whom little is known beyond the assertion that he was a skilled linguist. This small quarto in eights was printed as far as the end of signature E (p. 74) when the receipt of other poems, of which Marvell's is the first, necessitated the addition of a further signature and a half of text.

Shortly afterwards a second edition, dated 1650, was produced, the purpose of which seems to have been to obscure the division between the two sets of verse. This was only imperfectly achieved, and the principal changes made were the cancellation of the second list of contributors, the resetting of Marvell's elegy in consequence on a single bifolium, and its removal to an earlier position in the volume, among those of Herrick, Denham and John Hall. In bibliographical terms the move was unnecessary, and could in any case have been made to either of two other positions in the volume.

The inescapable conclusion seems to be that Marvell was given his natural place among his fellow poets. Herrick was then in London, moving in Inns of Court circles; Hall was at Gray's Inn, of which at least seven other contributors were members, and the fact may be of some significance as Marvell may have witnessed deeds there in 1642. Denham, however, was abroad with Charles II when he was invited to take part, while Marchamont Needham, whose verses followed Marvell's in the first edition, was in Newgate Jail for publishing *Mercurius Pragmaticus*.

29 **'*An* Horatian *Ode upon* Cromwell's *Return from* Ireland', about June or July 1650.**
C.59.i.8.

Cromwell returned from his subjugation of Ireland in May 1650 to take part in the Scottish campaign over which his superior, Fairfax, resigned in late June. Since the former General is nowhere mentioned, while Cromwell, seen as not yet 'grown stiffer with Command' (26 June), is about to lead his army against the Scots (22 July), the '*Ode*' was probably composed between these two dates, and before Marvell followed Fairfax into retirement. It was set up but cancelled before publication from all known copies of the folio but the present one and that in the Huntington Library: the anonymous compiler of the Bodleian copy supplied a manuscript version from which, together with the two other Cromwell poems, Thompson's text of 1776 was printed.

What the *Coy Mistress* is to Marvell's amatory lyrics the 'Horatian *Ode*' is to his political poems – simply his most perfect achievement. The basis of its excellence lies in Marvell's outstandingly balanced political outlook which could wholeheartedly admire the central figure of the new order while lamenting, at an interval of only eighteen months, the fate of his royal predecessor, secure in the conviction that all was for the best where destiny led. The ode is Horatian by virtue of the parallel that it affords with, for example, Horace's ode to Augustus after the battle of Actium (l. 37) and of its metre, which was used also by Richard Fanshawe and Thomas Stanley (see no. 23).

Easily the most famous passage in the '*Ode*' is Marvell's description (ll. 53–64) of the execution of Charles I, of which he may well have been an eye-witness. It is interesting to note that a contemporary Dutch engraving of the scene shows a mattress (cf. Marvell's 'Bed') by the block.

That thence the *Royal Actor* born
The *Tragick Scaffold* might adorn:
   While round the armed Bands
   Did clap their bloody hands.
He nothing common did or mean
Upon that memorable Scene:
   But with his keener Eye
   The Axes edge did try:
Nor call'd the *Gods* with vulgar spight
To vindicate his helpless Right,
   But bow'd his comely Head,
   Down as upon a Bed.

30 Lucan's *Pharsalia,* translated by Thomas May, 1627.

1068.i.6.

May's translation of the *Pharsalia* includes a passage about Caesar (Book 1, ll. 144 *et seq.*) that strikingly anticipates, and probably influenced, Marvell's equation of a victorious warrior with lightning breaking through clouds, together with other key terms to be found in the 'Horatian *Ode*' of summer 1650.

In view of this probable debt it would seem rather ungracious of Marvell to turn upon his poetic benefactor with the scathing satire entitled *Tom May's Death*, that must have been composed at some time after 13 November 1650. The case usually made out for his authorship of this posthumous attack is grounded in the assertion of his having fundamentally royalist sympathies, as yet unresolved into his later tenacious parliamentarianism. The evidence adduced in turn for this is his literary friendship with Lovelace of at least one year earlier, the sentiments expressed in the Villiers elegy of 1648 – itself only very doubtfully his work – and three fine stanzas on the courageous behaviour of Charles I on the scaffold.

Against this we may point out that *Tom May's Death* incorporates a thorough rejection of May's classicising bent that sorts ill with the recent 'Horatian *Ode*', in which Cromwell is explicitly compared to Caesar and Hannibal – to say nothing of some lines (ll. 141–4) in 'The Character of Holland' of February 1653; a condemnation of the 'apostacy' that, if we accept the customary biographical interpretation, Marvell himself might be thought pre-eminently guilty of; and the portrayal of Fairfax and Cromwell as '*Brutus* and *Cassius* the Peoples cheats'.

The attribution to Marvell of this satire, maintained in the face of every internal argument to the contrary, rests solely on the fact of its inclusion by Mary Palmer in the 1681 Folio: the piece was, however, deleted, together with 'Thyrsis and Dorinda', by the anonymous compiler of the Bodleian copy (see no. 52).

Koning Karolus de 2 Openlijck binnen Londen Onthalst

Dutch engraving of the execution of Charles I, 1649

Lyric Poet

Fair quiet, have I found thee here,
And Innocence thy Sister dear!
Mistaken long, I sought you then
In busie Companies of Men.
Your sacred Plants, if here below,
Only among the Plants will grow.
Society is all but rude,
To this delicious Solitude.

The Garden, st. II

THOMAS, Lord Fairfax, who in June 1650 resigned his command of the parliamentary armies to his lieutenant Cromwell, passed the next eight years in retirement in his native Yorkshire, collecting coins, medals and manuscripts, translating and composing verse, and improving his estates. These lay largely about the beautiful rivers Wharfe and Ouse, between his birthplace at Denton in the Pennines and his town residence at Bishophill in York, where his daughter Mary had been born. At the confluence of the rivers stood Nun Appleton, formerly a religious foundation, where Fairfax set about rebuilding the old house. Here Marvell spent one of the most placid and agreeable periods of his life, teaching languages to Mary Fairfax, enjoying rural pursuits and conversation with neighbouring members of her family, whose tastes were literary and antiquarian, keeping in touch with friends and relatives at Hull, and composing his own verses in praise of the Fairfaxes and the local countryside.

This interval of rural retirement provides a convenient excuse for considering some aspects of Marvell's lyrical achievement. That much of the lyric verse printed in *Miscellaneous Poems* (1681) belongs to this period is an assumption often tacitly entertained, though it is virtually certain that several pieces were composed at other times during the two decades following 1640, if not even later. It is interesting that Aubrey and Parker speak of his interest in poetry – not specifically satirical verse – as if it remained a preoccupation of his later years. At all events, to the tutorship in Yorkshire are attributable without doubt the three Fairfax pieces, by far the most important of them being the huge and discursive country-house poem *Upon Appleton House*, a rich quarry that includes family history, personal sketches and celebrations of the neighbouring fields, rivers and woods, together with more solemn reflections.

Of such pieces as are represented in the present exhibition by contemporary manuscript commonplace-copies the earliest, 'Thyrsis and Dorinda', is probably the only one of the three pastoral dialogues published in *Miscellaneous Poems* that is not actually by Marvell. Like many of his best pieces 'A Dialogue, between *the Resolved Soul and Created Pleasure*' belongs to an established poetic tradition, as does its counterpart the 'Dialogue between the Soul and Body': its arrangement and metrical scheme suggest a composition for musical setting, or even a short masque. Far enough removed from these is *Eyes and Tears*, a poem that consists of an ingenious set of conceits assembled in support of a paradoxical interpretation of its subject, and one that may perhaps belong to the same creative mood as *Mourning*. Finally, *To his Coy Mistress* represents the crown of Marvell's love-poetry, a perfectly-rounded syllogism whose simple logic is reinforced by easy transitions and resonant images. The recovery of these manuscript versions disproves the older notion that Marvell's lyric verse did not circulate during his lifetime.

Miniature portrait of Mary Fairfax
by Samuel Cooper, 1650 (31)

31 Miniature portrait of Lady Mary Fairfax by Samuel Cooper, 1650.
Duke of Buccleuch.

This miniature is one of two by Cooper in the Buccleuch collection to have been put forward as a portrait of Marvell's pupil, but as the features of the present sitter closely resemble those seen in portraits of Mary Fairfax when Duchess of Buckingham, in York City Art Gallery and Amyand House, the other, which shows a lady of less distinctive appearance, may be dismissed.

The present miniature, executed in water-colour on vellum, is signed and dated 1650; it must have been painted shortly before Mary's family left London for retirement at Nun Appleton. The image that it presents is of a plain-, even coarse-featured young woman, of whom Marvell, in the long passage dedicated to her in *Upon Appleton House* (sts. LXXXII–LXXXXVI), tactfully observed that '*She*, to higher Beauties rais'd, Disdains to be for lesser prais'd'.

Hence *She* with Graces more divine
Supplies beyond her *Sex* the *Line*;
And, like a *sprig* of *Misleto*,
On the *Fairfacian Oak* does grow;
Whence, for some universal good,
The *Priest* shall cut the sacred Bud;
While her *glad Parents* most rejoice,
And make their *Destiny* their *Choice*.

Her looks, in her thirteenth or fourteenth year, impart something of the robust good humour that would be needed to carry her through her marriage with the profligate second Duke of Buckingham. For their wedding in September 1657 Abraham Cowley wrote an epithalamium: two months later Marvell was to join Davenant in celebrating in verse that of Cromwell's daughter Mary, and we may perhaps ascribe his apparent silence on the former occasion rather to ignorance of the event than to his knowing how strongly Cromwell disapproved of the match.

32 Engraved portrait of Thomas, third Baron Fairfax, after John Hoskins, 1650.
B.M. Department of Prints and Drawings:
1885-2-14-44.

This fine engraving was made by C. H. Jeens about 1870 from a miniature portrait of Fairfax by Hoskins that was in 1903 in possession of C. P. Wykeham Martin of Leeds Castle, Kent. Its present whereabouts is unknown.

Hoskins' miniature was painted in the same year as Cooper portrayed Mary Fairfax, presumably that is in the spring or early summer of 1650, before Fairfax retired to his Yorkshire estates. He is not known to have left his place of retirement until in 1658 he journeyed to London to ask for the release of his son-in-law, the Duke of Buckingham, on which occasion he received a rebuff from Cromwell. Thurloe's spies at this period constantly reported him to be engaged in royalist intrigues.

In Richard Cromwell's parliament he sat for Yorkshire, voting with Haselrig and the opposition against Marvell's superior, and in November 1659 opened negotiations with Monck. His seizure of York in the following January facilitated Monck's passage into England and hence the Restoration. Parliament sent him to greet Charles at The Hague, but on the King's accession he retired once more to Nun Appleton.

Passages in *Upon Appleton House* and '*Upon the Hill and Grove at* Bill-borow' (st.IX) show that much as Marvell admired Fairfax in the pursuits of his retirement he could not forbear drawing a comparison with the glorious commander of the Parliamentary forces, shown in Marshall's famous equestrian portrait of 1645:

Much other Groves, say they, then these
And other Hills him once did please.
Through Groves of Pikes he thunder'd then,
And Mountains rais'd of dying Men.
For all the *Civick Garlands* due
To him our Branches are but few.
Nor are our Trunks enow to bear
The *Trophees* of one fertile Year.

BIBLIOGRAPHY: C. R. Markham, *The Life of the Great Lord Fairfax* (London, 1870); M. A. Gibb, *The Lord General* (London, 1938).

Engraved portrait of Thomas,
3rd Baron Fairfax,
after John Hoskins, 1650 (32)

33 Epigram 'Upon the new building at Apleton' by Lord Fairfax, about 1650-60.
Add. MS 11744, f.48.

The idea expressed in the opening lines of this epigram was a commonplace of the time, but may have been suggested by Marvell's verses in *Upon Appleton House*, st. IX:

The House was built upon the Place
Only as for *a Mark of Grace*;
And for an *Inn* to entertain
Its *Lord* a while, but not remain.

It seems likely, however, that Fairfax and Marvell are referring to different houses here.

This epigram is included in a manuscript of autograph fair-copies of original poems, translations and paraphrases composed by Fairfax and transcribed at some time after 1661. Besides several moral and religious epigrams, including one 'Upon the 30 of January on which the K was beheaded' (f. 42), there occur translations from Petrarch and of St Amant's *Les Solitudes* (ff. 72b-78b), a poem that seems to have echoes in

upon the new building
at Appleton

Think not ô man that dwells herein
This house was maid to stay at but as
an Inn
wch for accomodations fitly stands
In the way to manhions that's not maide
wth hands
But if a time here thou take thy rest
yett think on this Eternity's the best.

Autograph verses on Nun Appleton House by Lord Fairfax (33)

some of the verses that Marvell wrote during his period at Nun Appleton.

A larger autograph collection of poetry by Fairfax, entitled 'The Imployment of my Solitude', is now Bodleian MS Fairfax 40, and includes most of the pieces in the present manuscript. Yet another selection was to be found in a volume, now apparently lost, of materials relating to the family that was compiled in 1660 by Charles Fairfax of Menston, and was there headed 'Some Fruits of Vineyards, Gardens, and Orchards at Appleton'. It is mentioned in Thomas Thorpe's *Catalogue of Twelve Hundred Manuscripts*, 1832, lot 478; and another smaller version is now in the Brotherton Library at Leeds.

34 Engraved views of Nun Appleton House and Gardens by Daniel King, about 1655–60.
Harley MS 2073, f.126.

Daniel King (d. about 1661) had studied engraving under Hollar. His connection with the Fairfax family is attested by his dedication of *Miniatura, or the Art of Limning* (Add. MS 27362) to Mary Fairfax, before 1657, and of two engravings of Beverley Minster, published in his *Cathedrall and Conventuall Churches of England and Wales*, 1656, of which a copy survives in the present manuscript, to Lord and Lady Fairfax. His undated *Orthographical Designe of Severall Viewes upon the Road, in England and Wales* includes an engraving of Windsor Castle from a design by Fairfax's nephew Brian, and no doubt the vignettes of Appleton House and Gardens were inserted as a compliment to their owner and creator. It is not known exactly when the views were executed and published: it was clearly long enough after the 1637 edition of Camden's *Britannia*, to which the numbers on some of the individual plates refer, and the likeliest date is towards the second half of the decade 1650–60. It is difficult, however, to account for the portrayal of Bishophill as a ruin.

It has quite credibly been suggested that the house shown in King's views is not the one celebrated by Marvell in *Upon Appleton House*. The description given in stanza v of that poem is certainly inapposite:

Men will dispute how their Extent
Within such dwarfish Confines went:
And some will smile at this, as well
As *Romulus* his Bee-like Cell.

The old house that he loved had been erected with stones taken from the dissolved nunnery nearby (st. XI), and the famous and much-discussed stanzas (VI, VII) on the spherical hall may perhaps derive not from a boasted feature of new-fangled architecture but a sad lapse into near-ruin of the old structure.

BIBLIOGRAPHY: letters to the *Times Literary Supplement* of 26 November 1971; 28 January, 11 February and 31 March 1972.

Engraved views of Nun Appleton House and Gardens by
Daniel King, about 1655–60 (34)

From *Upon Appleton House*

LXXI.
Thus I, *easie Philosopher*,
Among the *Birds* and *Trees* confer:
And little now to make me, wants
Or of the *Fowles*, or of the *Plants*.
Give me but Wings as they, and I
Streight floting on the Air shall fly:
Or turn me but, and you shall see
I was but an inverted Tree.

LXXII.
Already I begin to call
In their most learned Original:
And where I Language want, my Signs
The Bird upon the Bough divines;
And more attentive there doth sit
Then if She were with Lime-twigs knit.
No Leaf does tremble in the Wind
Which I returning cannot find.

LXXV.
Then, languishing with ease, I toss
On Pallets swoln of Velvet Moss;
While the Wind, cooling through the Boughs,
Flatters with Air my panting Brows.
Thanks for my Rest ye *Mossy Banks*,
And unto you *cool Zephyr's* Thanks,
Who, as my Hair, my Thoughts too shed,
And winnow from the Chaff my Head.

LXXVI.
How safe, methinks, and strong, behind
These Trees have I incamp'd my Mind;
Where Beauty, aiming at the Heart,
Bends in some Tree its useless Dart;
And where the World no certain Shot
Can make, or me it toucheth not.
But I on it securely play,
And gaul its Horsemen all the Day.

LXXVII.
Bind me ye *Woodbines* in your 'twines,
Curle me about ye gadding *Vines*,
And Oh so close your Circles lace,
That I may never leave this Place:
But, lest your Fetters prove too weak,
Ere I your Silken Bondage break,
Do you, *O Brambles*, chain me too,
And courteous *Briars* nail me through.

LXXVIII.
Here in the Morning tye my Chain,
Where the two Woods have made a Lane;
While, like a *Guard* on either side,
The Trees before their *Lord* divide;
This, like a long and equal Thread,
Betwixt two *Labyrinths* does lead.
But, where the Floods did lately drown,
There at the Ev'ning stake me down.

LXXXI.
Oh what a Pleasure 'tis to hedge
My Temples here with heavy sedge;
Abandoning my lazy Side,
Strecht as a Bank unto the Tide;
Or to suspend my sliding Foot
On the Osiers undermined Root,
And in its Branches tough to hang,
While at my Lines the Fishes twang!

LXXXII.
But now away my Hooks, my Quills,
And Angles, idle Utensils.
The *young Maria* walks to night:
Hide trifling Youth thy Pleasures slight.
'Twere shame that such judicious Eyes
Should with such Toyes a Man surprize;
She that already is the *Law*
Of all her *Sex*, her *Ages Aw*.

35 Catalogue of the Reverend Henry Fairfax's books, after 1655.
Sloane MS 1872, ff.80b,81.

Henry Fairfax (1588–1665), uncle of Marvell's employer, was rector of Bolton Percy, the parish church of Nun Appleton, from 1646 until the Restoration, when he voluntarily retired to his private estate at Oglethorpe. In politics a moderate, Royalists and Parliamentarians alike were welcome at his rectory. His tastes ran from genealogy and antiquities to poetry of an extraordinarily wide range. He had been educated at Trinity College, Cambridge, where he was a contemporary and intimate friend of George Herbert.

Although *The Temple* surprisingly does not figure in his library, it included, besides dictionaries or grammars of nine oriental languages, literature in seven European languages – the learned tongues, Italian, French, Spanish and the vernacular – all of which were familiar to Marvell whose business it was to impart at least some of them to his pupil. Amongst them were the Latin odes of Casimir Sarbiewski, Tasso's *Amyntas*, Guarini's *Pastor Fido*, the poems of Ronsard and St Amant, a Rabelais, *Don Quixote*, the comedies of Lope de Vega and Corneille, the Latin sacred epigrams of Balduinus Cabilliavus ('Calzius'), the standard English classics and a few moderns such as Carew, Suckling and Herrick. Nun Appleton may have been remote from London society but retirement with such riches, both at the great house and the rectory, could not have been irksome to the young poet who was also an accomplished linguist.

36 'To his worthy friend Doctor WITTIE upon his Translation of the Popular Errours',
about winter 1650–1.
E.1227.

Robert Witty, a native of Beverley, was educated at Cambridge and between 1636 and 1642 filled the post of usher at Hull Grammar School. 'Popular Errours. Or the Errours of the People

in Physick' is his translation of a Latin work originally published in 1638 by James Primrose MD, a Frenchman of Scots extraction who had settled in the town, and under whose auspices Witty first began to practise medicine.

The dedication of the translation is dated 30 November and the preface 'From my house at *Hull*, Decemb. 2. 1650': George Thomason purchased the present copy on 3 May following. Those who contributed commendatory verses include at least two former pupils of Hull Grammar School besides Marvell, namely Anthony Stevenson, the Usher in Marvell's day, and two others who seem to have been at Trinity with the poet. All of these sign themselves *Art. Mag.*, while Marvell describes himself as 'A[ndreae] F[ilius]', an honourable enough title in Hull.

Marvell's two sets of verses were probably composed early in the winter of 1650–1. The English poem includes a flattering reference to '*Caelia*' who 'Now learnes the tongues of *France* and *Italie*' and is probably to be identified with Mary Fairfax, his pupil at Nun Appleton. A single correction of faulty scansion in the text of the Latin verses that was published in the Folio is the only evidence of serious revision by Marvell.

37 'A Dialogue between Thyrsis and Dorinda', copied about 1635–7.
Bodleian MS Rawl. poet. 199, pp. 52,3.

This charming pastoral dialogue was inserted almost as an afterthought in *Miscellaneous Poems*, 1681, and has generally been accepted as Marvell's; yet there are good reasons for questioning the ascription, with the compiler of the Bodleian copy who deleted it. The text of the poem is found in two principal versions, that of the Folio (which is very corrupt) corresponding with the one commonly encountered in printed and manuscript sources dating from the Restoration. The other version, which has an extended middle section (that is, the catalogue of heaven's delights, occupying ll. 21–38 of the Folio text) occurs in the Rawlinson manuscript and in a volume of musical settings composed by

William Lawes (d. 1645), and may be the earlier of the two.

The copying of the present manuscript, by a single transcriber, is closely associated with Christ Church, Oxford, of which many of the authors represented were members. None of the datable poems is known to have been composed after 1635: the dialogue itself is ascribed to Henry Ramsay who matriculated in June of that year, and whose name subsequently appears as contributor to various volumes of congratulatory verse issued by the University. Without accepting Ramsay as the author, and while allowing some latitude in the dating of the transcription, we may still feel disinclined to accept it as the work of a Cambridge undergraduate who had not yet attained his sixteenth or seventeenth year.

A version of the dialogue in its later form is seen in the 1663 edition of *A Crew of Kind London Gossips*, where it was printed directly from a manuscript copy dated 1653 in Cambridge University Library (Additional MS 79, ff. 19, 19b). This agrees with the Folio, except that between ll. 22 and 23 of the latter are inserted three couplets not found even in the fuller versions of Ramsay and Lawes. At all events this shows that the later recension was in existence at some time before or during 1653.

38 'Eyes & teares'.

Bodleian MS Tanner 306, f.388.

This transcript of the lyric composed 'by Mʳ. Marvil' occurs in a collection of loose copies of verse assembled by William Sancroft, a Cambridge graduate who became Master of Emmanuel and eventually Archbishop of Canterbury. The watermark of the leaf on which it is copied resembles one found by Edward Heawood (*Watermarks*, 1950, no. 1902a) in a London document of 1656. No editor has yet done justice to the half-dozen substantive and four accidental variants between this apparently early version and that published in the 1681 Folio, and it is interesting to note that the source used by the compiler of Bodleian MS Eng. poet, d. 49 in-

cluded three of these readings. Moreover, the omission of stanza IX from the Tanner version was not necessarily due to an oversight.

While still a junior member (about 1634–40) of Emmanuel, Sancroft transcribed a large selection of verse from Richard Crashaw's own manuscripts, showing a taste strange enough in the future head of a Puritan foundation but one that might account for his preservation, at a later date, of 'Eyes & teares', a poem that is often thought to have been prompted by Crashaw's elaborately-conceited rhapsodies on the tears of the Magdalen. This tends to be confirmed by the fact that Marvell chose to render stanza VIII – if indeed the Latin did not come first – into the mode of neo-Latin sacred epigram, of which Crashaw, whose *Epigrammatum Sacrorum Liber* was published at Cambridge in 1634, was certainly the most distinguished English practitioner. Vernacular models were provided by *The Weeper* and *The Teare*, published in *Steps to the Temple* (1646 and 1648), which Marvell may have read on his return from the continent.

The text that follows is that of the Bodleian version: common contractions have been silently expanded, and stanza IX has been inserted from the 1681 Folio for completeness' sake.

Eyes & teares

How wisely nature did agree
with the same eyes to weep & see!
That having view'd the object vaine
we might be ready to complaine.

And since the selfe-deluding sight
in a false angle takes each hight
These teares that better measure all
Like watry lines & plummets fall.

Two teares which sorrow long did weigh
within the scales of either eye,
And then paid out in equal poyse
as the true price of all my joyes.

What in the world most fair appear'es
yea even laughter turnes to teares
And all the jewels which we prize
melt in these pendants of the eyes.

I have through eve'ry Garden been
among the red, the white, the green.
And yet from all the flowers I saw
No honey but these teares could draw.

So the All-Seeing Sun each day
distills the world with Chymick ray
but finds its essence only showers
which streight in pitty back he powers.

Yet happy they whom greife doth blesse,
that weep the more & see the lesse.
And to preserve that sight more true
bathe still their eyes in their own dew.

So Magdalen in teares more wise
dissolv'd those captivating eyes,
whose liquid chaines could flowing meet
to fetter her Redeemers feet.

[Not full sailes hasting loaden home,
Nor the chast Ladies pregnant Womb,
Nor *Cynthia* Teeming show's so fair,
As two Eyes swoln with weeping are
                              1681 Folio]

The sparkling glance that shootes desire
drenchd in these waves doth lose its fire.
And oft the thunderer pitty takes,
& here his hissing lightning slakes.

The incense was to heaven deare,
not as a perfume but a teare.
And starres show lovely in the night
but as they are the teares of light.

Ope then mine eyes your double sluce
And practise so your noblest use;
for others too can see or sleepe,
but only humane eyes can weepe.

Now like two cloude's dissolving drop,
& at each tear in distance stop
Now like two fountaines tricle down
now like two floods ore'turn & drown.

Thus lett your stream'es oreflow your springs
Til eyes & teares be the same things
And each the others difference beares
These seeing eyes these weeping teares.

Magdala lascivos sic cum dimisit amantes
    fervidaque in castas lumina solvit aquas,
Haesit in irriguo lachrymarum compede Christus
    Et tenuit salvos uda catena pedes.

39 'A Combat Between the Soule And Sense'.
Bodleian MS Rawl. A. 176, f.80.

This manuscript version of the poem that was published in the *Miscellaneous Poems* of 1681 as 'A Dialogue, between *the Resolved Soul and Created Pleasure*' was salvaged by Samuel Pepys in September 1678 from among the papers left by the disreputable Captain James Scott in his former lodgings in Cannon Street. It is copied on a double sheet of paper which has suffered rather from being carried in the pocket: nevertheless it claims our attention as one of the very few commonplace-copies that are known of Marvell's lyric verse to be independent of the Folio.

Though there are frequent indications of unintelligent copying, some of the variant readings that it presents may demand our respect. The poem is often claimed, partly on the grounds of its metrical scheme, to have been written expressly with musical setting in mind: if the guess is a good one it renders more interesting the non-appearance in the present transcript of a couplet (ll. 15–16) that disturbs the regular quatrains of Pleasure's speeches, even though the notion expressed there is one of the most characteristically Marvellian touches in the piece:

Where the Souls of fruits and flow'rs
Stand prepar'd to heighten yours.

More significant at any rate is the title of the poem in this manuscript: here it is not merely a 'Dialogue' but a 'Combat', a description that is supported both by the persistent imagery of warfare and in the opening speech, unattributed in the Folio, but here shown to be the 'Charge' of the body to the soul on entering the lists against sensory delights.

BIBLIOGRAPHY: Elsie Duncan-Jones, 'A Great Master of Words: Some Aspects of Marvell's Poems of Praise and Blame' (British Academy Warton Lecture on English Poetry, 1975).

A Combat Between the Soule And Sense

Charge

Courage Courage My Soule now learn to wield
The weight of thy Immortall Sheild
Close on thy head thy helmet bright
Ballance thy sword against the fight
See where an Army strong as faire
With silken banners spread the aire
Now if thou bee'st that thing devine
In this dayes combat let it shine
And shew that nature wants an art
to conquer a resolved heart.

Sense

Wellcome the Creations Guest,
Lord of earth & heavens heire
Lay aside that warlike crest
And on natures banquet share.

Soule

I sup above & cañot stay
To bait soe long upon the way.

Sense

On these downy pillows lye
Whose soft plumes will thither fly
On these roses strow'd so plain
Least one leafe thy side should strain.

Soule

My Gentler rest is on a thought
Consious of doeing what I ought.

Sense

If thou bee'st with perfumes pleas'd
Such as oft the Gods appeas'd
Thou in fragrant clouds shalt show
like another god below.

Engraved emblem from Hermann Hugo's *Pia Desideria*, 1624
(40)

40 Hermann Hugo, *Pia Desideria*, Antwerp, 1624.

12305.aaa.37.

This moral and religious work in Latin by the continental Jesuit writer Hermann Hugo consists of prose homilies on selected texts from the Bible, rendered attractive to readers by the Latin poems and gracefully-executed plates accompanying each one. The plates were adopted by Francis Quarles for his own *Emblemes* (1635), but it is clear that Marvell was more familiar with Hugo's book, which was widely read in England. Two of the plates show a human soul locked in a cage and enclosed within a human skeleton, the latter (Book III, no. XXXVIII) having the motto *Quis me liberabit de corpore mortis huius?* (Who shall deliver me from the body of this death?). The former is accompanied by a poem in Latin elegiacs of which the first four couplets contain images elaborated by Marvell in the first stanza of his 'Dialogue between the Soul and Body':

Soul.

'O who shall, from this Dungeon, raise
A Soul inslav'd so many wayes?
With bolts of Bones, that fetter'd stands
In Feet; and manacled in Hands.
Here blinded with an Eye; and there
Deaf with the drumming of an Ear.
A Soul hung up, as 'twere, in Chains
Of Nerves, and Arteries, and Veins.
Tortur'd, besides each other part,
In a vain Head, and double Heart.'

Body.

O who shall me deliver whole,
From bonds of this Tyrannic Soul?
Which, strecht upright, impales me so,
That mine own Precipice I go;
And warms and moves this needless Frame:
(A Fever could but do the same.)
And, wanting where its spight to try,
Has made me live to let me dye.
A Body that could never rest,
Since this ill Spirit it possest.

Soul.

What Magick could me thus confine
Within anothers Grief to pine?
Where whatsoever it complain,
I feel, that cannot feel, the pain.
And all my Care its self employes,
That to preserve, which me destroys:
Constrain'd not only to indure
Diseases, but, whats worse, the Cure:
And ready oft the Port to gain,
Am Sipwrackt into Health again.

Body.

But Physick yet could never reach
The Maladies Thou me dost teach;
Whom first the Cramp of Hope does Tear:
And then the Palsie Shakes of Fear.
The Pestilence of Love does heat:
Or Hatred's hidden Ulcer eat.
Joy's chearful Madness does perplex:
Or Sorrow's other Madness vex.
Which Knowledge forces me to know;
And Memory will not foregoe.
What but a Soul could have the wit
To build me up for Sin so fit?
So Architects do square and hew,
Green Trees that in the Forest grew.

Had I but world enough, & tyme,
This Coynesse, Madam, were noe Crime.
I could sitt downe, & thinke which way
To walke, & passe our long-loues day.
You by y Indian Ganges side
Should Rubyes seeke, I by the Tide
Of Humber would complaine, I woud
Loue you ten yeares before y Floud,
And you should, if you please, refuse,
Till y Conuersion of the Iewes.
My vegetable Loue should grow
Vaster, then Empires, but more slow.
One hundred yeares should goe, to prayse
Your Brow, & on your forehead gaze;
Two hundred to adore your eyes,
But thirty thousand to your Thighes.
An age att least to euery part,
And the last Age to shew your heart.

For, Madam, you deserue this state,
Nor can I loue att lower Rate.
But harke, behind meethinkes I heare
Tymes winged Charriot hurrying neare,
And yonder all before vs lyes
Desarts of vast Eternityes.
Your beauty will stand neede of Salt,
For in the hollow Marble Vault
Will my Songs Eccho, Wormes must try
Your longe preseru'd Virginity.
Now then whil'st y youthfull Glue,
Stickes on your Cheeke, like Morning Dew,
Or like the amorous Bird of prey,
Scorning to admitt delay,
Lett vs all once our Selues deuoure,
Not linger in Tymes slow-Chopt power,
And synce Wee cannot make the Sun
Goe backe, nor stand, wee'l make him run.

Haward's version of *To his Coy Mistress* (41)

41 *To his Coy Mistress.*

Bodleian MS Don. b. 8, pp.283–4.

This is the only known text of Marvell's most famous lyric that is totally independent of the 1681 Folio, which it predates by some nine years. It occurs among a vast manuscript collection of miscellaneous prose and mainly satirical verse, compiled under a single cover by Sir William Haward of Tandridge, a Member of Parliament and Gentleman of the Privy Chamber to Charles II, whom Evelyn sneeringly called 'a greate pretender to English antiquities &c'. Haward's manuscript, which was transcribed between about 1667 and 1682, and includes several of Marvell's (supposed) satires, is a careful and even calligraphic compilation: the imperfections of this 'Poeme amorous' are probably attributable therefore to the copy from which he was working, and the date of transcription is almost certainly 1672. The year 1646 has been suggested for the poem's composition because of the reference to 'ten years before the Flood', the biblical event that was computed to have taken place *anno mundi* 1656.

Some of the readings here may survive from an earlier stage in the composition of the poem, but the most significant feature of the text is the first rhyme-word in the couplet 'Now then whil'st yᵉ youthfull Glue Stickes on your Cheeke, like Morning Dew' which is also that of the amended Folio in the Bodleian:

Now therefore, while the youthful glew
Sits on thy skin like morning dew . . .

The Folio itself reads 'youthful hew' and 'morning glew' and Marvell's first professional editor emended the latter to the smoother reading 'dew', which has met with general acceptance. However, the fact that the only three authoritative witnesses include the word 'glew' – the moisture that 'transpires/At every pore' and was recognised as a sign of youth and hot blood suggests that this was what the poet intended, and if so its natural position is as the first rhyme. A strikingly similar instance of editorial smoothing occurs in Thompson's edition at line 325 of *The First Anniversary*.

BIBLIOGRAPHY: Thomas Clayton, '"Morning Glew" and Other Sweat Leaves in the Folio Text of Andrew Marvell's Major Pre-Restoration Poems', *English Literary Renaissance*, II (1972), pp. 356–75.

To his Coy Mistress.

Had we but World enough, and Time,
This coyness Lady were no crime.
We would sit down, and think which way
To walk, and pass our long Loves Day.
Thou by the *Indian Ganges* side
Should'st Rubies find: I by the Tide
Of *Humber* would complain. I would
Love you ten years before the Flood:
And you should if you please refuse
Till the Conversion of the *Jews*.
My vegetable Love should grow
Vaster then Empires, and more slow.
An hundred years should go to praise
Thine Eyes, and on thy Forehead Gaze.
Two hundred to adore each Breast:
But thirty thousand to the rest.
An Age at least to every part,
And the last Age should show your Heart.
For Lady you deserve this State;
Nor would I love at lower rate.
   But at my back I alwaies hear
Times winged Charriot hurrying near:
And yonder all before us lye
Desarts of vast Eternity.
Thy Beauty shall no more be found;
Nor, in thy marble Vault, shall sound
My ecchoing Song: then Worms shall try
That long preserv'd Virginity:
And your quaint Honour turn to dust;
And into ashes all my Lust.
The Grave's a fine and private place,
But none I think do there embrace.
   Now therefore, while the youthful glew
Sits on thy skin like morning dew,
And while thy willing Soul transpires
At every pore with instant Fires,
Now let us sport us while we may;
And now, like am'rous birds of prey,
Rather at once our Time devour,
Than languish in his slow-chapt pow'r.
Let us roll all our Strength, and all
Our sweetness, up into one Ball:
And tear our Pleasures with rough strife,
Thorough the Iron gates of Life.
Thus, though we cannot make our Sun
Stand still, yet we will make him run.

42 Silvestro Pietrasanta, *De Symbolis Heroicis Libri IX*, Antwerp, 1634.

1327.b.11.

Pietrasanta (1590–1647), an Italian Jesuit priest who was a protégé of Flecknoe's acquaintance Cardinal Pier Luigi Carafa, became Rector of the College at Loretto, dying in Rome about a year after Marvell's visit there. He is thought to have been the first, in 1638, to differentiate between the colours in heraldic engravings by means of dots and hatching. His treatise of badges, emblems and *impressas* is illustrated with two hundred and sixty finely-engraved plates, the frontispiece being designed by Rubens.

The sixth chapter of Book VIII, on devising mottoes, includes the observation that the indicative mood is often used, *ut in Horologio ex horti deliciis consita, DOCET ET DELECTAT*. The accompanying plate shows a circular arrangement of flower-beds, each numbered as on the dial of a clock, with a central gnomon that throws a shadow from the sun around the face.

Such a pre-Linnaean garden-clock, bearing the same motto, is said to have existed in the garden of the Villa Aldobrandini in Rome. Marvell may have recalled it when composing the final verses of 'Hortus', the Latin counterpart of *The Garden*. In the English version, however, the basis of the conceit is almost entirely lost in a celebration of God's larger rural artefact.

How well the skilful Gardner drew
Of flow'rs and herbes this Dial new;
Where from above the milder Sun
Does through a fragrant Zodiack run;
And, as it works, th'industrious Bee
Computes its time as well as we.
How could such sweet and wholsome Hours
Be reckon'd but with herbs and flow'rs!

Floral horologue from Pietrasanta's
De Symbolis Heroicis Libri IX, 1634 (42)

Cromwell's
Laureate

'Tis Madness to resist or blame
The force of angry Heavens flame:
    And, if we would speak true,
    Much to the Man is due.
Who, from his private Gardens, where
He liv'd reserved and austere,
    As if his highest plot
    To plant the Bergamot,
Could by industrious Valour climbe
To ruine the great Work of Time,
    And cast the Kingdome old
    Into another Mold.
                'An Horatian *Ode'*, ll. 25–36

AT about the end of 1652 Marvell left the service of Fairfax and, with the support of Milton, applied for the post of assistant Latin Secretary in Whitehall. In its place he was offered a post as governor to Cromwell's protégé and prospective son-in-law William Dutton, whom he accordingly accompanied to Eton that summer. There they lodged, by Cromwell's wish, in the house of John Oxenbridge, a puritan Fellow of the College, whose reminiscences of the Bermudas, where he had spent two periods of religious exile, prompted Marvell's poem of that title. Whilst there Marvell made the acquaintance of the musician and poet Nathaniel Ingelo and, at nearby Ritchings, of John Hales. To the former, who soon after departed in the suite of Cromwell's Ambassador to Sweden, he addressed a long verse-epistle in Latin, the political nature of which is as marked as that of '*The First* Anniversary of the Government under *His Highness* the Lord Protector', which followed almost a year later, in December 1654.

Nothing is known of Marvell's affairs during 1655, but by January 1656 he was abroad with his charge, at Saumur on the Loire, where there was a famous Protestant academy. He remained there until at least August of that year, being described by a visiting Royalist as a 'notable English Italo-Machavillian', and returned to England probably no later than the following January. The subsequent gap in our knowledge of his movements lasts until the autumn, and is filled only by his composition, at some time during the spring or summer, of the little-admired verses '*On the Victory obtained by* Blake *over the* Spaniards'. After September his Secretaryship in Whitehall kept him fairly busy, though he had energy to spare for further verses in commendation of the House of Cromwell, celebrating with two songs the marriage of the Protector's third daughter to Lord Fauconberg (sometimes rendered Fauconbridge) in November. In September of the next year he had the melancholy task of lamenting the death of Cromwell, whom for more than eight years he had not merely admired and served but had come to love.

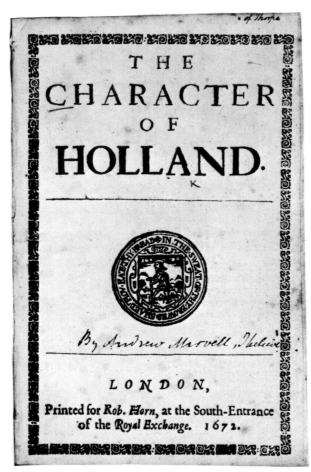

Title-page of 'The Character of Holland', 1672 (44)

... there will be with you to morrow upon some occasion of busines a Gentleman whose name is Mr Marvile; a man whom both by report, & the converse I have had with him, of singular desert for the State to make use of; who alsoe offers himselfe, if there be any imployment for him. His father was the Minister of Hull & he hath spent foure yeares abroad in Holland, France, Italy, & Spaine, to very good purpose, as I beleeve, & the gaineing of those 4 languages; besides he is a scholler & well read in the Latin and Greeke authors, & noe doubt of an approved conversation, for he com's now lately out of the house of the Lord Fairefax who was Generall, where he was intrusted to give some instructions in the Languages to the Lady his Daughter. If upon the death of Mr Wakerley the Councell shall thinke that I shall need any assistant in the performance of my place . . . it would be hard for them to find a Man soe fit every way for that purpose as this Gentleman . . .

Surprisingly enough, Milton's testimony is the only independent corroboration that we have of Marvell's connection with the Fairfaxes outside his lyric poems. In the event he had to wait four and a half years before he was appointed to a similar post in Whitehall, in which he was occasionally called upon to deputise for Milton.

BIBLIOGRAPHY: J. Milton French, *Life Records of John Milton*, vol. III, pp. 322–4 (New Brunswick, 1954).

44 'The Character of Holland', about February 1653.
C.71.h.13.

Marvell's satire on the Dutch, which includes details doubtless observed during his stay there in the 1640s, was composed most probably soon after the English naval victory off Portland on 18–20 February 1653. It thus belongs to an intensely interesting and important period of his career, namely that between the interview with Bradshaw on 22 or 23 February, and his appointment as governor to Cromwell's ward-to-be in the early spring or summer. Though it includes no specific mention of Cromwell its celebration of the Commonwealth suggests perhaps that Marvell was putting himself forward as official verse-propagandist of the new state:

43 Milton's letter to John Bradshaw, 21 February 1653.
Public Record Office SP 18/33, no.75.

Writing to the President of the Council of State, to which he acted as Latin Secretary, Milton recommends Marvell for the vacant post of assistant in the same office. The letter was dictated to an amanuensis, since Milton had been totally blind for about a year, and runs in part:

For now of nothing may our *State* despair,
Darling of Heaven, and of Men the Care;
Provided that they be what they have been,
Watchful abroad, and honest still within.
(1681 Folio, ll.145–8)

In this role he would not be competing with his sponsor Milton, whose last poem of that nature – the sonnet on Cromwell – was written during the previous May, and whose energies were increasingly taken up with prose controversy. Ultimately Marvell came to be looked on over the next six years by the Protector as his own laureate.

The full text of Marvell's satire was not published until the *Miscellaneous Poems* came out in 1681. However, on 13 June 1665, ten days after the English victory at Solebay, the poem was entered by Robert Horn in the Stationers' Register, being issued without Marvell's final fifty-two verses, which related too closely to the earlier period, but with an eight-line conclusion suitable for the new campaign. No copy of that edition is now known, but during the Third Dutch War in 1672 Horn again seized on the poem's topicality and brought out the present pamphlet.

Portrait of William Dutton of Sherborne (45)

45 Portrait of William Dutton of Sherborne.

Sherborne Court, Gloucestershire: photograph by courtesy of The Connoisseur.

Dutton's father was a Royalist who died shortly after the surrender of Oxford in 1646, leaving him an orphan in the care of his wealthy uncle John Dutton of Sherborne Court, Gloucestershire. By an agreement with this uncle Cromwell was, on the former's death, to assume guardianship of the youth, who was to inherit the Sherborne estate, making him a suitable match for Cromwell's youngest daughter, Frances. As preparation for the future, William's education was forthwith entrusted to Cromwell, who appointed Marvell his governor and sent them to live at Eton in June 1653. There they remained for at least two years, moving to Saumur at some time shortly before January 1658 and returning to England most probably on the death of John Dutton in the following January.

The style of dress adopted by the sitter, traditionally identified as William Dutton, in this portrait from Sherborne Court does not perhaps, any more than the pose, testify to the success of his supposedly Puritan upbringing. Writing to Cromwell at the beginning of his tutorship, however, Marvell described his charge (see no. 46) as 'of a gentle and waxen disposition . . . . He hath in him two things which make Youth most easy to be managed, Modesty which is the bridle to Vice, and Emulation which is the Spur to Virtue.' What seems to make the attribution more likely is Marvell's reference to his pupil's unhealthy complexion, which is faithfully shown in this portrait.

BIBLIOGRAPHY: Leonard Willoughby, 'Sherborne House', *The Connoisseur*, XXX, pp. 3–13 (May 1911); [Blacker Morgan], *Historical and Genealogical Memoirs of the Dutton Family, of Sherborne* (privately printed, 1899).

Marvell's Latin epigram on Cromwell's picture sent to Sweden, about 1653–4 (47)

46 Marvell's letter to Cromwell, 28 July 1653.
Society of Antiquaries of London MS 138 p. 152.

Marvell wrote to Cromwell as soon as he had settled in at Eton with Cromwell's protégé, whom he accompanied there as governor or moral tutor. Dutton would no doubt receive formal tuition in academic subjects within the College; Marvell's principal tasks were to watch over his welfare, 'to increase whatsoever Talent he may have already' according to Cromwell's rules for his conduct, 'to set nothing upon his Spirit but what may be of a good Sculpture', and 'to make him sensible of his Duty to God'. To promote this latter end Cromwell had placed them both in the household of a recently-elected Fellow of Eton, John Oxenbridge, a noted preacher whose puritanism had caused him to seek a refuge in the Bermudas from Laud's persecution. To Dutton's governor Oxenbridge's 'Doctrine and Example are like a Book and a Map . . . demonstrating . . . which way we ought to travel': Marvell's lyric celebration of the Puritan spirit in *Bermudas* evidently took its rise from that example. As for Mrs Oxenbridge's care of Dutton, 'She has lookd so well to him that he hath already much mended his Complexion: And now she is busy in ordring his Chamber . . .' These touches picture to us the very model of a homely, puritan household.

Bermudas

Where the remote *Bermudas* ride
In th' Oceans bosome unespy'd,
From a small Boat, that row'd along,
The listning Winds receiv'd this Song.
    What should we do but sing his Praise
That led us through the watry Maze,
Unto an Isle so long unknown,
And yet far kinder than our own?
Where he the huge Sea-Monsters wracks,
That lift the Deep upon their Backs.
He lands us on a grassy Stage;
Safe from the Storms, and Prelat's rage.
He gave us this eternal Spring,
Which here enamells everything;
And sends the Fowl's to us in care,
On daily Visits through the Air.
He hangs in shades the Orange bright,
Like golden Lamps in a green Night.
And does in the Pomgranates close,
Jewels more rich than *Ormus* show's.
He makes the Figs our mouths to meet;
And throws the Melons at our feet.
But Apples plants of such a price,
No Tree could ever bear them twice.
With Cedars, chosen by his hand,
From *Lebanon*, he stores the Land.
And makes the hollow Seas, that roar,
Proclaime the Ambergris on shoar.
He cast (of which we rather boast)
The Gospels Pearl upon our Coast.
And in these Rocks for us did frame
A Temple, where to sound his Name.
Oh let our Voice his Praise exalt,
Till it arrive at Heavens Vault:
Which thence (perhaps) rebounding, may
Eccho beyond the *Mexique Bay*.
Thus sung they, in the *English* boat,
An holy and a chearful Note,
And all the way, to guide their Chime,
With falling Oars they kept the time.

47 Marvell's Latin epigram on Cromwell's portrait sent to Sweden, about 1653–4.
Add. MS 34362, f.41.

Cromwell's portrait is sometimes said to have been sent to Queen Christina during the year 1653 or 1654, but no record of the presentation has been found other than in this epigram and the tradition that attaches to two such portraits, one at Gripsholm Castle in Sweden and the other at Chequers. The fact that Whitelocke's account of the embassy to Sweden, which took place between November 1653 and 1654, makes no mention of Cromwell's gift may mean that it had been made previously. The artist was almost certainly either Robert Walker or Samuel Cooper.

These lines were claimed for Milton by John Toland in 1698, but their close relation to the Latin distich on Cromwell's portrait that is certainly by Marvell, and to the Ingelo poem, as well as (to a lesser extent) their inclusion in the 1681 Folio, leaves little doubt that they are indeed Marvell's. It is also worth remarking that Milton was totally blind by about February 1652.

The epigram is attributed to Marvell in the present beautifully copied manuscript also, which seems to have been transcribed mainly between Marvell's death and the publication of the Folio, of which, however, its texts are quite independent. It includes eight poems and one prose piece that have been or still are attributed to Marvell, and in 1661, before transcription, belonged to a Samuel Danvers: two cousins of that name, both born about 1636, were tradesmen in London in the 1670s. The manuscript subsequently belonged to Sir Thomas Phillipps, and was acquired by the British Museum at Sotheby's sale of 21 June 1893 (lot 626).

BIBLIOGRAPHY: F. N. Macnamara, *Memorials of the Danvers Family* (London, 1895).

48 'A Letter to Doctor *Ingelo*, then with my Lord *Whitlock*, Ambassador from the *Protector* to the Queen of *Sweden*', about the winter of 1653–4.

152. f.5.

In November 1653 Nathaniel Ingelo, a linguist, musician and something of a poet, whom Marvell had met at Eton a few months earlier, was chosen to accompany Bulstrode Whitelocke as chaplain and *rector chori* on the embassy that Cromwell was sending to arrange a political and commercial treaty with Sweden. To him Marvell addressed the longest and most classically

formal of his Latin poems, which, despite its ostensibly personal occasion, is no less than a plea in support of the alliance: it was certainly intended for the eye of the learned Queen Christina, whom it flatters at length. In a passage full of classical allusions (ll. 25–58) Marvell describes her portrait, which he must have seen in the Protector's closet at Whitehall. From a few details that can be accepted as literal the portrait-type has not yet been identified, though it may have resembled that of Erik Parise's medal which dates from this period.

Portrait medallion of Queen Christina by Erik Parise, about 1650–5 (48)

Portrait medallion of Bulstrode Whitelocke
by Abraham Simon, 1653–4 (48)

There is every reason to think that the idea of writing the poem was Marvell's own, but it probably received Cromwell's sanction. No exact date has been set to its composition, though it may just possibly be identified with one of the Latin poems that Whitelocke showed the Queen on 30 March 1654. The Ambassador himself comes in for no praise, not even receiving a mention, unless we accept the punning reference in the description of Godfrey of Bulloigne at his coronation, *Spina cui canis floruit alba Comis* ('on whose *white locks* flourished the white thorn'). His own exhaustive account of the embassy, however, survives in manuscript, and his appearance at this time is shown in a medal executed by Abraham Simon, a protégé of the Queen.

The text shown here occurs in the second volume of Jean Arckenholtz's *Mémoires concernant Christine*, 1751–60, which includes the first half only of Marvell's poem, there entitled *ANGELO SUO MARUELLIUS*. It is printed from a manuscript copied by Jean Scheffer, one of the savants employed by Christina, and seems therefore likely to be an accurate witness to the version that was actually read by the Queen.

This differs in some respects from that published in the Folio, notably in its inclusion of an extra couplet accidentally omitted there.

49 '*The First* Anniversary Of The Government Under *His Highness* The Lord Protector', 1654–5.
E.480(1).

Cromwell was made Protector on 16 December 1653. Marvell's poem, written for the following December and probably sent privately to its dedicatee was taken up by the government, being set up by their printer for use as propaganda. It was not entered in the Stationers' Register, but was advertised in *Mercurius Politicus*, no. 240, for 11–18 January 1654/5: the present copy bears the purchase date of 17 January added in manuscript by the bookseller George Thomason. Cromwell seems to have used some phrases from the poem in the speech with which he dismissed Parliament at the end of that month.

This edition, a quarto of twenty-four leaves, must probably stand as the best witness to the text of the panegyric, and it was reprinted from the quarto with a very few minor variants in the 1681 Folio, from which, however, it was cancelled in all but the British Library copy (C.59, i. 8). The manuscript version supplied in Bodleian MS Eng. poet. d. 49 (see no. 52) seems again to be taken from the quarto, though with minor differences mainly of paragraphing; while Thompson's text of 1776, which incorporates some of the variants encountered in the Bodleian copy along with many more unsupported and unsupportable readings of the same kind as occur in his texts of the other two Cromwell poems, was probably based on Popple's manuscript, with corruptions and emendations. Finally, two other manuscript texts, in B. L. Burney MS 390 and Bodleian MS Eng. poet. e. 4, like *Poems on Affairs of State*, 1707, ascribe the poem to Edmund Waller, and E. S. Donno reposes much confidence in the readings of this second Bodleian version.

In this poem, while Marvell delivers a sustained and sincere encomium upon Cromwell's

fitness to be Protector of the Realm, he nevertheless stops short, like Cromwell himself, of
kingship, if only for the time being:

Hence oft I think, if in some happy Hour
High Grace should meet in one with highest Pow'r,
And then a seasonable People still
Should bend to his, as he to Heavens will,
What we might hope, what wonderfull Effect
From such a wish'd Conjuncture might reflect.
Sure, the mysterious Work, where none withstand,
Would forthwith finish under such a Hand:
Fore-shortned Time its useless Course would stay,
And soon precipitate the latest Day.
But a thick Cloud about that Morning lyes,
And intercepts the Beams of Mortall eyes,
That 'tis the most which we determine can,
If these the Times, then this must be the Man.
And well he therefore dos, and well has guest,
Who in his Age has always forward prest:
And knowing not where Heavens choice may light,
Girds yet his Sword, and ready stands to fight . . .

(ll. 131–48)

Miniature portrait of Cromwell
by Samuel Cooper, 1656 (50)

50 Miniature portrait of Oliver Cromwell by Samuel Cooper, 1656.

National Portrait Gallery: cat. no. 3065.

Cooper is known to have been working for
Cromwell and his family as early as 1650, and it
is possible that the superb unfinished *ad vivum*
sketch in the Buccleuch Collection was made as
early as that date. The Buccleuch miniature is
said to have served as the original of copies made
for official presentation after Cromwell became
Protector in December 1653.

The Latin epigram that Marvell composed
on the portrait of Cromwell that was sent to
Sweden in 1653 or 1654 cannot certainly be
identified with the Cooper type. The distich 'In
Effigiem *Oliveri Cromwell*', undated but possibly earlier than the other, speaks not of its
subject's war-scarred face and terrible aspect
but of his '*Umbra*' – meaning simultaneously,
the portrait itself, the Protector's shadow and
his spectre.

Haec est quae toties Inimicos *Umbra fugavit,*
At sub qua Cives *Otia lenta terunt.*

BIBLIOGRAPHY: Daphne Foskett, *Samuel Cooper*,
pp. 74–6 (London, 1974).

51 Letter of James Scudamore to Sir Richard Browne; Saumur, 15 August 1656.

Add. MS 15858, f.135.

Scudamore, the fourth son of John, first Viscount Scudamore of Sligo, had been granted a
pass to travel abroad in the previous December;
his correspondent, Sir Richard Browne, was
then Charles II's resident at Paris. To him
Scudamore reported from Saumur that 'Many
of the English are here but few of Noate such
onely are The Lord Pagets sonne, [and] M^r
Dutton calld by the french Le Genre du
Protecteur whose Governour is one Mervill a
notable English Italo-Machavillian. I will not
trouble you with a Catalogue of the rest they
being either inconsiderable in their fortunes or
age to be capable of acting anything serviceable.'
Evidently Marvell did not scruple to express
political opinions similar to those that underlie
the 'Horatian *Ode*' in his private conversation.
It is possible that Scudamore was advised on
this point by Paget's tutor, Joseph Williamson,

Saumur: 15. August 1656.

Sir:

I shall nee more. pinne my faith upon
any of St Bernards relations for a certaine post, since I finde
Father stapleton of that order has proud soe bad a presenter
of my letter with my seruice to you; He pretended to mee soe
familiar acquaintance with you, that I was confident I
had hitt on the right channell for the conueyance of my
respects vnto you, but I confesse now I was too credulous an
obseruer of his sacred robe, wch ill successe you will please
to pardon, & admitt I beginne againe to kisse your hands
by the opportunitie of this gentlemans passage who assures
mee of confirming that my desire by the deliuery of this.
To tell you any thing of the place of Saumur were as Impor=
=tinent as to discourse to you of Paris, since no scituation of
france but is perfectly knowne to you. Many of the English
are here but few of Noate such onely are The Lord Pagets
sonne, Mr Dutton call'd by the french Le Genre du Protecteur
whose Gouernour is one Meruill a notable English Italo=Macha=
=uillian. I will not trouble you with a catalogue of the rest
they being either inconsiderable in their fortunes or age to
be capable of acting any thing seruiceable. Wee are very
dead as to any newes here, and most of these parts are as
apt to forgett as to be sorry for what happned at Valentienne

Be pleased to looke ouer |

who had lived at Saumur since January 1655, taking pupils, and must have met Marvell socially following the latter's arrival late in that year.

Though clearly an intelligent and lively observer Scudamore was a rash character and in February of the next year was imprisoned at Paris for non-payment of debts. By a strange irony Dutton, whose claim to fame at Saumur resided in the proposed match with Cromwell's daughter Frances, found himself supplanted by Robert Rich and subsequently married Scudamore's sister Mary.

BIBLIOGRAPHY: Pierre Legouis, 'Saumur as Marvell saw it', *Aspects du XVIIe siècle*, pp. 63–76 (Paris, 1973).

52 'A Poem upon the Death of His late Highnesse the Lord Protector', about September–November 1658.

Bodleian MS Eng. poet. d. 49, p. 150.

Cromwell died at Whitehall on 3 September 1658, the anniversary of his two great victories at Dunbar and Worcester, and the day after the great storm. His body was embalmed and displayed in state at Somerset House from 20 September: Marvell saw it most probably at this time, and may have completed his elegy before the funeral on 23 November, in which he took part. On 20 January following Henry Herringman entered it in the Stationers' Register, together with verses by Dryden and Thomas Sprat, but when the volume appeared, under another imprint, a piece by Waller that had previously been issued in a broadside was used instead.

The elegy was set up, presumably from Marvell's autograph copy, in the *Miscellaneous Poems* of 1681 but was wholly cancelled before publication, along with the two other Cromwell poems, from all but the British Library copy (C.59.i.8) which, however, preserves only verses 1–184. The remainder of the text was supplied in Thompson's edition of 1776 from what is now Bodleian MS Eng. poet. d. 49, a copy of the 1681 Folio that comprises manuscript

corrections and revisions in, as well as excisions from, the printed part, and continues with inserted texts of the Cromwell poems and seventeen post-Restoration satires. The final two satires, added in a different hand from the rest, were subsequently ascribed to Marvell's friend John Ayloff and crossed through.

The hand of the principal copyist of the Bodleian Folio appears to belong somewhere within about three decades of Marvell's death, but the identity of the compiler and the authority attaching to his emendations, additions and deletions have occasioned considerable debate among recent editors. Margoliouth was surely right to identify this compilation with the 'manuscript volume of poems written by Mr. William Popple, being a collection of his uncle Andrew Marvell's compositions after his decease' that he had received for the purpose of his edition from T. J. Mathias. Though the handwriting nowhere resembles Popple's own the hand that added the extra translation by Sir Philip Meadows of the lines from Seneca on p. 63 compares quite well with that of his son William (d.1722), the father of the dramatist (cf. Bodleian MS Locke c. 17, f. 267). The elder William Popple, whose official correspondence at the Board of Trade was commonly transcribed by clerks, may have adopted this method for copying his uncle's poetry.

If nothing else, the agreement in several instances of the substitutions made in the printed part of the volume with some that occur in contemporary commonplace copies (see nos. 38, 39 and 41) suggests that the compiler was not merely emending wilfully, but had other witnesses by him; and the fact of his apparently seeking to attribute ultimate authority to these copies must mean either that they were autograph or that they derived at least from the author himself. Nevertheless, if he intended an improved text of the poetry he does not seem to have allowed for Marvell's frequent habit of revision: the readings that he substituted in two of the Latin pieces make no more and no less sense than the printed ones, and need have suggested themselves to no one but the poet: they must therefore survive from an earlier stage of composition.

From the little evidence that survives, then, we may most probably assume that the texts of the lyric poems left by Marvell among his papers represent his final thoughts, but that the compiler of the Bodleian copy, probably his nephew William Popple, knew better than Mary Palmer which of the pieces found in his hand or at any rate in his closet were actually of his composition. This argument may not, however, apply in all respects to the satires.

53 Wax death-mask of Oliver Cromwell, 1658.

B.M. Department of Medieval and Later Antiquities: O A. 4276

The British Museum death-mask was taken after embalment, but before the eyelids needed propping up, as is shown by the cloth used to cover the cincture made when the skull-cap was removed, and by comparison with the Ashmolean mask. The features are recognisably those of the Protector, as shown in the portraits, with flowing moustache, small beard and nose inclined to the left, though the wart over the right eye has been pared off.

For students of Marvell's poetry a specific interest attaches to Cromwell's physiognomy because of its handling in the Latin lines on the portrait sent to Queen Christina (see no. 47) and the following passage (ll. 247–254): from the poem on Cromwell's death (see no. 52)

> I saw him dead, a leaden slumber lyes
> And mortall sleep over those wakefull eys:
> Those gentle Rayes under the lidds were fled
> Which through his lookes that piercing sweetnesse
>   shed:
> That port which so Majestique was and strong
> Loose and depriv'd of vigour strech'd along:
> All wither'd, all discolour'd, pale and wan,
> How much another thing, no more that man?

BIBLIOGRAPHY: Karl Pearson and G. M. Morant, *The Portraiture of Oliver Cromwell* (London, 1935).

54 Marvell's participation in Cromwell's funeral procession, 23 November 1658.

Lansdowne MS 95, f.41b.

Cromwell's magnificent funeral was originally intended for 9 November, but owing to the great preparations necessary was deferred until Tuesday 23rd. At an early stage a list was drawn up of the persons who were to take part in the procession, grouped according to their offices: the individual sections were subsequently disposed in their relative positions following the hearse, and each was alloted a room in Somerset House in which to assemble. The third section, which was to form in the Privy Chamber, included:

> Secretarys of the French & Latin Toungs.
> M[r] Dradon   M[r] Sterry
> M[r] Marvell   M[r] John Milton
> M[r] Hartleb sen:[r]
> M[r] Pell (*subsequently deleted*)
> M[r] Bradshaw (*deleted*)

The first four of these had on 7 September been granted 9s 6d each – 9s only in Dryden's case – by the Council of State, with which to buy mourning.

The procession moved from Somerset House along the Strand and down Whitehall to Westminster Abbey, where Cromwell's effigy was laid in state, the corpse itself being removed privately to Henry VII's Chapel at an unknown date. £60,000 were allowed for the ceremony, of which £19,000 were still owing in the following August. On 30 January 1661, the anniversary of Charles I's execution, Cromwell's corpse was exhumed and hanged at Tyburn, the body then being buried under the gallows and the head set up on Westminster Hall where it remained until 1684.

BIBLIOGRAPHY: J. Milton French, *Life Records of John Milton*, vol. IV, pp. 235,6;244,5 (New Brunswick, 1956).

No more shall follow where he spent the dayes
In warre, in counsell, or in pray'r, and praise,
Whose meanest acts he would himself advance
As ungirt David to the Arke did dance.
All All is gone of ours or his delight
In horses fierce, wild deer, or armour bright.
Francisca faire can nothing now but weep
Nor with soft notes shall sing his cares asleep.

I saw him dead, a leaden slumber lyes
And mortall sleep over those wakefull eys:
Those gentle Rayes under the lidds were fled
Which through his lookes that piercing sweetnesse shed:
That port which so Majestique was and strong
Loose and depriv'd of vigour stretch'd along:
All wither'd, ill discolour'd, pale and wan,
How much another thing, no more that man?
Oh humaine glory vaine, Oh death, Oh wings,
Oh worthlesse world, Oh transitory things.

Yet dwelt that greatnesse in his shape decay'd
That still though dead greater then death he layd.
And in his alter'd face you something faigne
That threatens death he yet will live againe.

Not much unlike the sacred Oake which shoots
To heav'n its branches and through earth its roots:
Whose spacious boughs are hung with Trophees round
And honour'd wreaths have oft the Victour crown'd.
When angry Jove darts lightning through the Aire
At mortalls sins, nor his own plant will spare

J+

Civil Servant

. . . for as to my self, I never had any, not the remotest relation
to publick matters, nor correspondence with the persons then
predominant, until the year 1657, when indeed I enter'd into
an imployment, for which I was not altogether improper, and
which I consider'd to be the most innocent and inoffensive
toward his Majesties affairs of any in that usurped and irre-
gular Government, to which all men were then exposed. And
this I accordingly discharg'd without disobliging any one
person, there having been opportunity and indeavours since
his Majesties happy return to have discover'd had it been
otherwise.

The Rehearsall Transpros'd, Part II

IN his reply to Parker's allegation Marvell was essentially speaking the truth: as Cromwell's employee at Eton and Saumur he had had no direct part to play in the government until September 1657, when he finally achieved his earlier ambition and was appointed Latin secretary in the office of John Thurloe at a salary of two hundred pounds a year.

As secretary to the Council of State and head of the overseas intelligence service Thurloe was one of the most powerful men in the government: he was, moreover, an admirer and intimate friend of the Protector. Marvell's duties under him included translating correspondence and official papers from and into Latin, receiving on occasion envoys from foreign states, and probably acting as interpreter. From time to time he was called upon to deputise for Milton, at whose house in Petty France he was a constant visitor.

Under Richard Cromwell Marvell retained his Secretaryship, though he was elected joint Member of Parliament for Hull in January 1659. In May, on the collapse of Richard's government and the restoration of the Rump he merely forfeited his seat, while Thurloe fell altogether from power, his offices being taken over largely by the regicide Thomas Scott. For Marvell life under this inveterate opponent of the Cromwells may not have been entirely happy: nevertheless he continued in his post, even being granted lodgings in Whitehall, until at least October 1659, when the Council of State was dissolved.

Gold portrait medallion of John Thurloe
by Thomas Simon, 1653 (55)

55 Gold portrait-medallion of John Thurloe, 1653.

*B.M. Department of Coins and Medals:
M.I.,1,406/40.*

This very rare and beautiful medallion of Thurloe in his early days as secretary to the Council of State was chased and cast, with a ring for suspension, by Thomas Simon from a model by his brother Abraham. It bears a bust of Thurloe, who is in profile, facing right, with long hair, a cap on his head, a plain falling collar and wearing a close buttoned doublet. The reverse has a double cipher composed of his initials, under which occurs the legend 'Secr. Thurloe'.

Thurloe owed his own earliest preferment to Oliver St John, under whom in March 1651 he was granted a position during the embassy to Holland, while St John's own appointment was celebrated by Marvell, then tutor at Nun Appleton, in some Latin verses. From December 1652 he was head of the government's intelligence service and in May 1655 took control both of inland and foreign posts. His loyalty to the House of Cromwell was absolute; besides being numbered among Oliver's personal friends he had helped him to the Protectorship and was anxious for him to accept the crown. Under Richard Cromwell his power even increased, but in April 1659 he unsuccessfully advised Richard against dissolving Parliament. By May of the same year Thurloe was out of office and remained so until the following February when he enjoyed a brief return to power. At the Restoration the offer of his services was rejected by Charles II and he found himself imprisoned for a time on a charge of high treason. On his release he divided his time between his house in Oxfordshire and his chambers at Lincoln's Inn, where he died in February 1668.

56 Richard Newcourt's map-view of London and Westminster, 1658.

Map Library: Maps 183.p.1(4).

This engraved bird's-eye view of the capital as it was during the Commonwealth period was 'Ichonographically described by Richard Newcourt of Somerton in the County of Somerset Gentleman. Willm Faithorne Sculpsit'. Newcourt's eight-sheet map, though larger than any of its predecessors, at a scale of about twelve inches to the mile, fails to distinguish any individually recognisable buildings in the manner achieved by earlier cartographers and by Hollar in his view of London shortly before the Fire. Two exemplars of the original engraving are known, that in the Bibliothèque Nationale being the only complete one.

Though the details are hardly to be relied upon Newcourt shows the north side of Cowcross, where Marvell had lodged sixteen years earlier. The street was perhaps more accurately

portrayed in a map-view of about 1591 that has been ascribed to Ralph Agas, and again in the Hollar engraving mentioned above.

Newcourt's representation of the Palace of Whitehall is probably more reliable. It was the principle residence of Cromwell, and also housed officials of the government, like Thurloe, who was to lose his lodgings there in the following year, on the fall of Richard Cromwell. In July 1659 Marvell, then working under Thomas Scott, was granted lodgings there, but it is not known when he relinquished them.

In March 1669 Marvell appears to have been lodging at the Crown by Charing Cross, at the top of Whitehall, on the site of the present no. 15, hard by Old Scotland Yard where lived Sir William Haward, the transcriber of *To his Coy Mistress* (see no. 41).

BIBLIOGRAPHY: I. Darlington and J. Howgego, *Printed Maps of London* (London, 1964).

57 'The Justice of the Swedish Cause and the danger of the Protestant Cause involved therein', 'by Monsr Frezendorp', about January 1658.
Add. MS 4459, ff.184b,185.

Marvell's longest known autograph manuscript comprises forty neatly-transcribed pages of translation – his own, we may be sure, from Latin – of a political tract attributed to the Swedish envoy in England, Johann Frederick von Friessendorff. This is accompanied in the volume of Thomas Birch's collections in which it occurs by a letter (ff. 194–195b) that dates from some time between 20 January and 4 February 1658, since it mentions what must have been the second session of Cromwell's second Parliament.

As the tract was aimed at persuading the Protector to lead his navy and that of Sweden against Holland and Spain this conjectural dating, and the success of the attempt, receives apparent confirmation from a draft that survives elsewhere in Thurloe's hand of the heads of a treaty for a defensive and offensive alliance with Sweden that is dated 25 March following (*Thurloe's State Papers*, vol. VII, pp. 23, 24).

58 Cromwell's letter to the Marquess of Brandenburg, 18 February 1658.
Bodleian Rawl. MS A 57, f.358b.

This letter, copied in Marvell's hand shortly after Cromwell had dissolved Parliament and begun to rule alone, was written from one head of State to another, demanding punishment for the treatment meted out by one of Brandenburg's naval commanders to the master of the 'Thomas of Ipswich' in May 1657. As such it would in normal circumstances have been rendered by Milton, the principal Latin Secretary, into the language of official correspondence, as had two letters to Brandenburg of the preceding August and September. Milton's second wife had died on 8 February, but even if we may assume that grief temporarily unfitted him for his duties, this would not entirely account for the gap that occurs in his Latin letters of state between 18 December 1657 and 30 March following: further search may reveal how far Marvell deputised for Milton in this area.

The English version preserved here may have been taken down at Cromwell's dictation but more probably at that of John Thurloe, and the style shows that it was written with translation in mind. We may feel confident that it was Marvell who rendered it into the Latin version printed in *Thurloe's State Papers* (vol. VI, p. 812).

desire you, or rather require according to your own
justice that you would represse and chastise the
violence and insolency of your men, as contrary
and destructive to the Common Law of nations, the
security of Commerce, and our mutuall confederacy.
And that you would comand full satisfaction to
be given to the Plaintiffe. For, as we are very
desirous to cultivate your friendship, which we
highly value, so on the other side, we neither can
nor ought to be wanting to our ~~subjects~~ people imploring
Our Protection. Given at Our Palace of Westminster the 18th of February In the yeare 165 7/8

Your good friend

O: P:

To the most Serene &c: the
Marquis of Brandenburg &c:

Cromwell's letter to Brandenburg, 1658 (58)

Juxta hoc Marmor, breve Mortalitatis speculum,
Exuviæ jacent Janæ Oxenbrigiæ.
Quae nobili, si id dixisse attinet,
Paterno Butleriorum, materno Claveringorum genere orta,
Johanni Oxenbrigio Collegii Ætonensis socio nupsit.
Prosperorum deinceps & adversorum Consors fidelissima.
Quem religionis causâ oberrantem,
Usque ad incertam Bermudae Insulam secuta:
Nec Mare vastum, nec tempestates horridas exhorruit:
sed, delicato Corpore,
Quos non Labores exantlavit? quae non obivit Itinera?
Tantum Mariti potuit Amor, sed magis Dei.
Tandem cum, (redeunte conscientiarum libertate) in patriam redux,
Magnam partem Angliæ cum Marito pervagata;
Qui laetus undequaque de novo disseminabat Evangelium.
Ipsa maximum ministerii sui decus,
& antiqua modestia
Eandem animarum capturum domi, quam ille foris exercens,
Hic tandem divino nutu cum illo consedit:
Pietatis erga Deum, charitatis erga proximos,
Conjugalis & materni affectus, omnium Virtutum
Christianarum Exemplum degebat inimitabile.
Donec quinque annorum hydrope laborans,
Per lenta incrementa ultra humani corporis modum intumuit.
Anima interim spei plena, fidei ingens,
stagnanti humorum diluvio tranquillè vehebatur.
Et tandem post 37 peregrinationis annos, 23 Apr. Aº 1658
Evolavit ad Cœlos tanquam Columba ex Arcâ Corporis:
Cujus semper dulci, semper amaræ memoriæ,
Mœrens Maritus posuit.
Flentibus juxta quatuor liberis,
Daniele, Bathuo, Elizabetha, Maria.

In a faire marble stone nigh a north chappell a black
marble yt had an inscription now covered wth paint.

Juxta hoc marmor breve mortalitatis speculum
exuviae jacent Janae Oxenbrigiae
Quae nobili, si id dixisse attinet
Paterno Buthriorum, materno Claveringorum genere [orta]
Johanni Oxenbrigio Collegij Etonensis socio nupsit
Prosperorum deinceps et adversorum consors fidelissima
Quem religionis causa oberrantem
Usque ad incertam Bermudae insulam secuta
Nec mare vastum, nec tempestates horridas exhorruit
Sed delicato corpore
Quos non labores exantlavit, quae non obivit itinera
Tantum mariti potuit amor, sed majus dei
Tandem cum redeunte conscientiarum libertate in patriam [redux]
Magnam partem Angliae cum marito pervagata
Qui latus undequaque de novo disseminabat evangelium

59 Marvell's *Janae Oxenbrigiae Epitaphium*, early summer 1658.

Lansdowne MS 1233, f.99.

Marvell composed this epitaph while a Latin secretary in Whitehall, for inscription on the monument to the first wife of John Oxenbridge, in whose house at Eton he had lodged with William Dutton. Jane Oxenbridge died on 23 April 1658 and her monument was placed in the Chapel, near the entrance to Lupton's chantry; it was removed during the extensive alterations of 1699. The present transcript, made on 8 May 1661, when the black marble had been white-washed over by royalists, is included in a collection of epitaphs taken from churches up and down the country by an unknown copyist. It comes closest to what must have been the actual form of the inscription, which was arranged line by line according to the periods, and not as continuous prose, as it was printed in the *Miscellaneous Poems* of 1681 from a draft preserved by the author.

Several other early manuscript copies derive from a careless transcript made by a Chapel clerk at Eton, which was faulty in some of its readings; however, comparison of these with the versions set out in the Lansdowne manuscript enables us to recover the actual form of the inscription and to discover that it differed in several minor details from that printed in the Folio. Like the Trott epitaphs the Folio text was evidently set up from a draft or fair-copy taken by Marvell before the final changes were made. A conjectural reconstruction is shown here beside the manuscript.

BIBLIOGRAPHY: W. H. Kelliher, *loc. cit.*

New Palace Yard with Westminster Hall and the Clock House by Hollar, 1647

60 Marvell's letter to George Downing, 11 February 1659.

Add. MS 22919, f.78.

The script of the present letter is a beautiful example of Marvell's middle-period hand – stylish yet easily legible, as befitted a Latin Secretary. Its open, rounded appearance is the result, like nineteenth-century copperplate that to some extent it resembles, of a steady control exercised in its formation; but in his later years it declined into the over-generously spaced and exaggerated hand shown in the letter to Harley (see no. 100). By 1659 also the uncertainties of the earlier signatures had been resolved into a style that is perfectly consistent with the hand as a whole, as is shown for example in the characteristic initial capitals.

Marvell's letter was written at the request of 'Mr Secretary' Thurloe, who was 'something tired with Parliament and other businesse', to the English diplomatic agent at the Hague. Richard Cromwell's Parliament, which had been convened on 27 January 1659, was computed to contain two hundred friends and only fifty overt enemies of the new Protector. On 1 February Thurloe, as the official head of Richard's supporters, had introduced a bill for full recognition of the Protectorship, the debate on the second reading of which is related here. Among the opponents of the bill was the regicide Thomas Scott, shortly to become Marvell's head of department and subsequently to be executed at the Restoration: he said of Richard that 'if you think of a single person, I would sooner have him than any man alive', but persisted in challenging the grounds of his authority. The opposition tried every possible delaying tactic, but Marvell saw that 'our justice our affection and our number . . . wil weare them out at the long runne', and on 14 February the bill was passed, though with a few amendments, by 223 votes to 134.

At the Restoration Downing, who in 1657 had been among those who tried to make Cromwell king, dexterously made his peace with Charles II. Two years later, to show his zeal, he arrested three regicides and sent them back to England where they were executed shortly before Marvell travelled to Holland to stay, perhaps with Downing, at the Hague. Pepys commented that 'All the world takes notice of him for a most ungrateful villain for his pains': Marvell's feelings, though nowhere betrayed, may be guessed at.

78

Sir,

Mr Secretary being something tired with Parliament
and other business hath commanded me to giue you
some account of what hath passed in the house this
weeke. Upon Munday the Bill for recognition of his
Highnesse was red the second time. Thereupon the House
entered into that debate And all hath been said against
it which could be by Sr Arthur Haslerig, Sir Henry Vane,
Mr Weauer, Mr Scott, Mr St Nicholas, Mr Reinolds, Sr
Antony Ashly Cooper, Major Packer, Mr Henry Neuill
and many more. Their Doctrine hath moued most upon their Maxime that all pow'r is in the people. That
it is reuested into this house by the death of his Highnesse, that Mr Speaker is Protector in possession and it
will not be fit wisdome to part with it easily, that this
house is all England. Yet they pretend that they
are for a single person and this single person but without
negatiue voice without militia not upon the petition
and aduice but by adoption and donation of this House
and that all the rights of the people should be specifyd
and indorsed upon that Donation. But we know well
enough what they mean. A Petition from some thousands
in the City to their purpose hath been brought in & they say,
they are trying to promote another in the Army, but laid
by to be red at the end of this debate in which nothing
is to interuene. They haue held us to it all this weeke
and yet little nearer. It was propounded on our side seeing
the whole bill stuck so, that before the Commitment of it
it should be voted in the house as part of it that his Highn
is Protector &c: and not to passe but with the whole bill.
But all we could gaine hitherto is that their shall be a
preuious vote before the Commitment but yt that should
be it is yet as farre of as euer. For they speake eternally to
the question, to the order of the house, and in all the
tricks of Parliament. They haue much the odds in speaking but it is to be hoped that our justice our affection
and our number which is at least two thirds will weare

Whitehall Febr: 11:
1658

Andrew Newport

In your most humble and
most faithfull seruant

tyre you out at the long running. This is all that I can
tell you at present but that I am—

the lord Lambton

We having taken into consideration that
during our interruption a certain treaty of
the 21 May ~ 59 concerning some affaires of
moment relating to the Commonwealth of England to France & to the United Provinces
was held at the Hague between the most
Excellent &c: Mr de Thou &c: George Downing &c: under the name & title of English
Resident but ~~now our Commissioner to~~
~~the states Generall~~ & the Lords John

Baron of Ghent &c:

Consideratione habitâ quod durante Nostrâ
interruptione Tractatus quidam vicesimi pri-
mi Maij Anno Millesimo Sexcentesimo quin-
quagesimo nono de rebus quibusdam magni momenti
ad Rempublicam Angliæ, Galliam, et Ordines
Generales Unitarum Belgij Provinciarum pertinentibus Ha-
gæ Comitum instituttus fuerit inter Illustris-
simum & excellentissimum &c: Jacobum Geor-
giam Downing Armigerum suis nomine et titulo Residentis
illic Anglici ~~nunc autem Commissarij nostri~~
~~ad Celsos et præpotentes Ordines Generales et Unita-~~
~~rum Belgij Provinciarum~~, et Dominos Johannem
&c:

61 'Forme of the Ratification of the Treaty at the Hague as it is passed under the Greate Seale', about 30 June 1659.

Bodleian Rawl. MS A 66, f.15.

In May 1659, following Richard Cromwell's dissolution of the Parliament in which Marvell himself sat for Hull, Thurloe had fallen from power: his functions were largely taken over by Thomas Scott, the regicide, who had preceded him as head of the intelligence service. It is difficult to believe that Marvell could have enjoyed working under this ferocious republican and opponent of the House of Cromwell, or that Scott, if he knew of them, would have been very happy about his secretary's Oliverian affiliations. On the other hand, the grant of lodgings in Whitehall that the Council of State made to Marvell at some time on or before 14 July suggests that his efficiency had made him acceptable to those in authority.

In the summer of 1659 Marvell seems once more to have deputised for Milton in transcribing, on a single sheet of paper, an English formula for ratification of the Commonwealth's treaty with the States General, together with his draft of it into Latin, incorporating *currente calamo* revisions.

62 Engraved portrait of James Harrington by Hollar, after Lely, 1658.

B.M. Department of Prints and Drawings: Cracherode P4–224.

James Harrington (1611–77), although in principle a republican, is said to have been deeply shocked by the execution of Charles 1, with whom he had discussed political and other questions in the Isle of Wight. In 1656 he printed his *Commonwealth of Oceana* which was dedicated to Cromwell, after whose death he formed 'The Rota', a club for the discussion of political theories, which met from November 1659 to February 1660. Members or auditors included Cyriak Skinner, Henry Neville and John Aubrey, while Marvell himself is said to have spoken there. It came to an end when the Restoration was in prospect, and in November 1661 Harrington's fortunes changed. After a spell of

Engraved portrait of James Harrington by Hollar, 1658 (62)

imprisonment he was attacked by periodic bouts of insanity, which, however, did not prevent him marrying. During the latter part of his life he lived in the Little Ambry at Westminster, where he died on 11 September 1677.

Aubrey, who describes him as, rather like Marvell, of middling stature, strong, well-set, with 'quicke hot-fiery hazell eie [and] thick moyst curled haire' says that the poet 'made a good epitaph for him, but [it] would have given offence', that is, to the ruling political hierarchy or the Court. Aubrey also remarks that in his younger days he made 'severall essayes in Poetry, viz. love-verses, etc. . . . but his muse was rough' and he was disuaded 'from tampering in poetrie'.

Portrait medallion of Charles II
by Pieter van Abeele, 1661

Member for Hull

It is true that by reason of so many Prorogations of late years repeated, the Publick businesse in Parliament hath not attain'd the hoped maturity; so that the weight and multiplicity of those affairs at present will probably much exclude, and retard at lest, any thing of more Private and particular consideration. Yet if any such you have, I shall strive to promote it according to the best of my duty: and in the more generall concerns of the nation shall God willing maintaine the same incorrupt mind and cleare Conscience, free from Faction or any selfe-ends, which I have by his Grace hitherto preserved.

Letter to Hull Corporation, 18 January 1677

O N the restoration of the Rump Marvell's seat had been taken by another, but in April 1660 he was elected to the Parliament that recalled Charles II, and was ironically given the task of answering in Latin a letter of congratulation received on that occasion. In November begin the letters – nearly three hundred surviving from what must have been an even larger number – that he wrote to Hull Corporation, reporting on the progress of their particular interests and on parliamentary business in general; while a parallel series was addressed, from May 1661, to Hull Trinity House, on whose behalf he also exerted himself until his death.

Between June 1662 and January 1665 Marvell, while retaining his seat, was absent almost continuously from the House and the country at the instance of the Earl of Carlisle. The first occasion was a political mission to Holland, concerning which nothing is known: in July 1663 he set out again as private secretary to Carlisle who had been appointed 'Embassadour Extraordinary to Muscovy, Sweden and Denmarke'. In Moscow Carlisle's brief was to secure the restoration of privileges to English merchants at Archangel: on several occasions Marvell met the Tsar Alexis, and engaged in wrangles concerning protocol with the Russian officials, but in the end the mission proved fruitless.

The next event of importance in Marvell's political career was his involvement in the campaign against Clarendon which led to the former Chancellor's impeachment in October 1667, and to his flight soon after. At this period, and during the rule of the Cabals over the next six years, his closest affiliations were with the Duke of Buckingham, leader of the Country Party and errant husband of his former pupil, Mary Fairfax. Their names are even linked with that of Captain Blood in an informer's report of September 1671. Buckingham had the credit of proposing to the King the Declaration of Indulgence of the following March, hailed by Marvell in *The Rehearsal Transpros'd*, but this was repealed within the year and the Test Act was introduced by the Commons.

At this juncture Sir Thomas Osborne rose to power, and the famous story of the proposed bribe originated during the remaining five years of Marvell's life. Marvell, who had withdrawn all his hopes from the King after his failure to carry through his policy of toleration, had strong reasons for disliking those of Osborne, a vigorous supporter of the Anglican establishment. On 27 March 1677 the Member for Hull, who is said to have spoken seldom in the House, made his longest speech that has come down to us, against the 'Act for further securing the Protestant religion' which would have increased the power of the bishops, the enemies, as he saw it, of religious toleration. This and the subsequent sessions of Parliament in 1677 were described in his *Account of the Growth of Popery and Absolute Government*, and, with the King defeated in his demand for a vote of supply to aid the States General against France, Parliament was again prorogued in the following June. Two months later Marvell was dead.

63 The Nettleton portrait of Marvell, about 1657–62.

National Portrait Gallery: cat. no.554.

This lively painting by an unknown artist must be accepted as an authentic likeness since it is clearly related to, and may have served as the immediate model for, the engraving that forms the frontispiece to *Miscellaneous Poems* (1681): if so we may reasonably infer that it was in Marvell's possession at his death. At a later period it passed to the Nettleton family, and in 1764 the poet's great-nephew Robert Nettleton, who set up the memorial tablet in St Giles's Church, presented it to the British Museum, whence it was transferred in 1879 to the National Portrait Gallery. The portrait, in oils on canvas, measures $23\frac{1}{2} \times 18\frac{1}{2}$ inches.

Marvell, who in stature was a 'thick, short man' (see no. 71), is portrayed much as Aubrey remembered him from his attendance at Harrington's Rota Club, or later, that is to say 'pretty strong sett, roundish faced, cherry cheek't, hazell eie, browne haire'. The luxuriance of this latter feature is striking: that his hair was his own and not a wig is shown by his wearing a skull-cap to draw attention away from probable thinning at the crown. Though in the latter half of the century most men preferred to go clean-shaven, a thin moustache had come into vogue

after the death of Charles I, which persisted throughout the reign of his son. Marvell's close-fitting buff jerkin is set off by a falling band in the form of a bib, its edges meeting at the front, and revealing underneath the tasselled band-strings. A striking resemblance in dress and pose is offered by Daniel King's engraved self-portrait (see Harley MS 2073, f.76b), which is dated 1658. Dress and features combine to indicate that the sitter was about forty years old, and we may therefore fairly ascribe it to some time between September 1657, when he took up a post in Whitehall, and June 1662, after which date he was abroad almost continuously until January 1665.

BIBLIOGRAPHY: D. Piper, *Catalogue of Seventeenth-Century Portraits in the National Portrait Gallery*, pp. 221–2 (Cambridge, 1963); C. W. and P. Cunnington, *Handbook of English Costume in the Seventeenth Century*, (London, 1972).

64 The Hollis Portrait of Marvell, about 1662.

Hull Museums.

Among the many portraits that have been claimed as likenesses of Marvell, whose features seem to have been by no means unique in his

ANDREW
AET SV

age, a high place must be awarded to the Hollis portrait. This is known to have been among the collections assembled by the Yorkshire antiquary Ralph Thoresby (1658–1725), after whose death it came indirectly into the hands of the republican and connoisseur Thomas Hollis (1720–74). Hollis is known to have proposed an edition of Marvell's works, and in 1760 had the portrait engraved by Cipriani: in 1776 it was engraved again, by Basire. The original, an oils on canvas measuring $18\frac{3}{4} \times 22\frac{1}{2}$ inches, was presented to Hull Corporation in 1921 by F. A. Page-Turner, a direct descendent of the poet's sister, Anne Blaydes.

An inscription on the portrait reads 'ANDREW MARVELL AET SVAE 42', which would set it between March 1662 and March 1663: unless it was painted in Holland we may reduce these limits to March and June 1662, if the inscription is correct. At all events the portrait would be roughly contemporary with that in the National Portrait Gallery (see no. 63), though as a work of art it does not rank as highly as the others, the poor skill of the artist giving a rather shifty look to the eyes and mouth. An alternative view was given, however, by Thomas Hollis in a letter written to a friend: 'If Marvell's picture does not look so lively and witty as you might expect, it is from the chagrin and awe he had of the Restoration then just effected. Marvell's picture was painted when he was forty-one; that is, in the year 1661 (as appears under the frame) in all the sobriety and decency of the then departed Commonwealth.'

BIBLIOGRAPHY: D. Piper, *op. cit.*, pp.221–2.

65 Engraved portrait of Charles Howard, first Earl of Carlisle, by Faithorne, 1669.

B.M. Department of Prints and Drawings:
Cracherode P5–96.

During the Civil War Howard (1629–85), despite initial suspicion of royalist sympathies, distinguished himself on the parliamentarian side at Worcester. In 1653 he was appointed to the Council of State, and in the following year made captain of the Protector's body-guard. Cromwell summoned him to his House of Lords in December 1657, and in April 1659 Howard urged Richard to arrest the army leaders, being himself imprisoned after the collapse of the Protectorate. Notwithstanding his role under the Commonwealth he was on Charles's return made a Privy Councillor and created Earl of Carlisle.

Carlisle and Marvell had probably met in Whitehall while the former belonged to the party of Richard Cromwell's supporters, which was headed by John Thurloe. Marvell's letter to Trinity House of 8 May 1662 announces his intention of visiting Holland by 'the interest of some persons too potent for [him] to refuse', amongst whom Carlisle alone is named. He was subsequently employed as Carlisle's private secretary during the long embassy to Russia, Sweden and Denmark, which lasted from July 1663 to January 1665. Another member of the party, Guy de Miège, published a *Relation of Three Embassies* (1669), in which the present portrait appears as a frontispiece.

66 Guy de Miège. *A Relation of Three Embassies* 1669.

1056.a.34.

Carlisle and his train set out across Russia by sledge in the depths of the winter of 1663/4. After being kept waiting outside Moscow, which they entered on 6 February, the Ambassador asked his secretary to draw up an official letter of complaint to the Tsar. In a subsequent oration before Alexis, whom he addressed as *Illustrissimus* and not *Serenissimus*, Marvell offended the Russians, but made an eloquent reply to their objections. All these documents are printed by Miège. The embassy left Moscow on 24 June 1664 with nothing accomplished. On 4 January following they had just left Hamburg when the following incident occurred, which shows Marvell's hot temper: he had evidently not learned discretion since the time that he exchanged blows with Thomas Clifford in the precincts of the Commons, in March 1662.

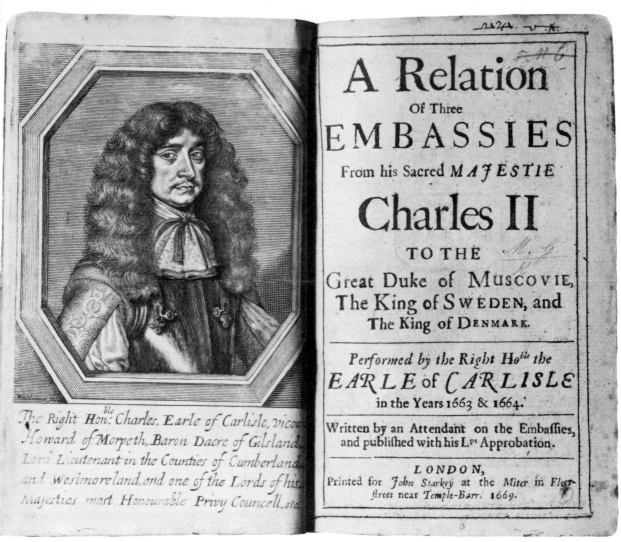

Guy de Miège, *A Relation of Three Embassies*, 1669, with Faithorne's engraved portrait of the Earl of Carlisle (65, 66)

The same day we departed from *Hamburg*, we were surprized with an accident at *Bockstoud*, a Town depending on the Crown of *Sweden*. For being upon the point of departing after dinner, and having hired fresh waggons to make three or four leagues that night, it hapned that the Secretaries wagoner would not stir, unless there might go along with him another wagoner his Comrade, who would have been as useless to us as his waggon. The Secretary not able to bring him to reason by fair means, tried what he could do by foul, and by clapping a pistol to his head would have forced him along with him. But immediately his pistol was wrested from him, and as they were putting themselves into a posture to abuse him, we interposed so effectually, that he was rescued out of the hands of a barbarous rout of peasants and Mechanicks.

67 The Earl of Carlisle's letter to Henry Bennet, 14 June 1664.
Public Record Office: SP91/3, f.107.

This letter was written from Moscow immediately after Carlisle's final audience with the Tsar. Having reported the failure of his mission in a letter to Charles II, Carlisle then dictated another to Marvell 'For Mr Secretary Bennett' (later Earl of Arlington and protector of Marvell's printer), in which he expressed his indignation more freely: 'What else was to be expected in a country where all other beasts change their colours twice a yeare but the rationall beasts change their soules thrice a day . . .

Or what Privileges could Merchants hope for
where Embassadors must all depart from
theirs.'

Two days later the Tsar sent a present of
sables, to be distributed among the
ambassador's train according to rank, but
Carlisle, says Miège, 'considering he had been
neglected in all his affaires, would by no meanes
admit of this obligation; but from a generous
principle returned the Present . . .' Miège also
notes the dismay of Carlisle's followers at this
juncture, adding, however, that 'we could not
for all that forbear praising the generosity of his
Conduct'.

68 Marvell's letter to the Mayor and Corporation of Hull, 26 October 1667.
Hull City Archives: BRL 2758

This letter includes Marvell's earliest in-
timation to his constituents of one of the most
important parliamentary events of Charles II's
reign, and one moreover in which he himself
was an actor. In the interval between the parliamentary sittings that ended in July and began
anew in October 1667 the King decided, on
account of Clarendon's growing unpopularity
both with the Court party and the country at
large, to remove him from the lord chancellor-
ship. Accordingly the Great Seal was demanded
and given up on 30 August. The Commons
when they met set up, on 17 October, a committee to enquire into the conduct of the Second
Dutch War, appointing Marvell one of its members. On the day on which the present letter was
written they resolved to arraign Clarendon of
high treason.

Though Marvell might write as often as three
times a week to the Corporation while the House
was in session, of the 295 letters that survive
from his Parliamentary career none is known to
have been preserved from six of the nineteen
mayoralties between 1659–78. This in itself
suggests that, while his descriptions of political
affairs are bland enough, the missing letters
were destroyed by their recipients as potentially
incriminating: it is interesting that none survives from Richard Cromwell's Parliament or
from the whole period of the Parker controversy.

69 Marvell's speech concerning Clarendon's impeachment, 6 November 1667.
Add. MS 33413, f.40.

The parliamentary diary of John Milward
(1599–1670), Member for Derbyshire, which
covers the period from September 1666 to May
1668, includes one of the more trustworthy ac-
counts of the proceedings during Clarendon's
impeachment. Milward had been active for
the King in the early part of the Civil War,
at the Restoration was named as one of the
deputies to William Cavendish, Earl of De-
vonshire, the Lord Lieutenant of Derbyshire,
and took his place in the House of Commons on
the date that the diary begins. The party to
which he belonged were Cavaliers, and he
would have had little in common with 'Mervin'
– the misnomer shows that they were not well
acquainted – beyond a probable hatred of
Popery.

In the debate on the articles of Clarendon's
impeachment drawn up by the committee appointed for that purpose on 26 October 1667
Marvell had an exchange with another Member
over the terms of the indictment. Milward re-
ports it thus: 'After all the Articles of the charge
had bin debated Mr Mervin pressed that the
words that were said to be spoken against the
King should not be passed over in silence but be
declared, the words as it sayd are these (The
Chancellor should say that the King was an
unactive person and indisposed for government
. . .' The witness to this remark of Clarendon's
was then traced back through Sir John Denham,
the poet, to 'another who would Justifie' it. One
may, however, feel slightly uncomfortable on
Marvell's account for the attempt to add this
final straw to the former Chancellor's load.

70 'The names of such as may bee ingaged by the Duke of York and his friends', about September 1669.
Add. MS 28091, f.148.

The name of 'Mr Marvell' occurs as one of those
who might be favourably inclined to the Duke of
York in a list drawn up by Sir Thomas Osborne
probably in September 1669, shortly before
Parliament reconvened. Osborne's patron

~~Resolued vppon ye queston~~
~~vppon ye mayne queston~~
~~the noes~~

Sr Wm Country
Sr Ro.t Barnham
Coll: Kirby
Mr Otway
D Gorge
Mr Leigh
Sr Tho: Allen
D Richardson
Sr Ralph Hare
Sr Hen yelu.rton
Sr Tho: Crew
Mr Ant: Eyre
~~Sr ....~~
Sr Jo: Mallett
Mr Glascock
Mr Oglander
Sr Jo: Holland
Sr Tho: Clarges
Sr Tho: Woodcok
Mr Col.man
Mr Low
Sr Jo: Earnley
Sr Lieu.t Braham
Sr Jo: Goodrick
Mr Burwell
Sr Frederick Hide
Mr Roger Pepys
Mr Harwell
Sr Jo: Country
Sr Ralph Banks
Sr Jo: Frgonwell
Sr Kirkford
— In all — 45

D ffawley
Sr Rich: Powell
Sr Jonathan Trelawny
~~Sr ....~~
Mr Wren
Mr Oxonill
Mr Roger Vaughan
~~Sr ....~~
Sr Allen Apsley
~~.........~~
Sr Allen Broderick
Mr Thurland ——— In all — 9

~~In mayne to the queston yesterday~~
~~ye affirmative the oldfloored~~
~~the nose dismiss Tuesday~~

Sr Tho: Dolman
Sr Lieu.t Ingoldsby
Mr Cheney
Mr Crouch
Mr Arundell
Mr Tho: Country
Sr Hen: Vernon
Mr Anchitell Grey
Mr Cullisford
Sr Jo: Brampston
Sr Hen: Capell
Mr Dowdeswell
Sr Tho: Peyton
Mr Bullitt

Buckingham, the leader of the Country Party, was about to propose an alliance with the Court Party and the remaining Clarendonians, his purpose being to secure a vote of supplies for the government by making some concessions to Catholics and Dissenters. Osborne forecasted success on the calculation that the Commons included ninety-two government officials, nine servants of the Duke of York, with a further forty-five members who might be called upon by him and his friends, thirty-nine supporters of Buckingham and one hundred and six others who had already shown willingness to incline to the government. This would have made up a handsome majority, though in the event no such coalition took place.

It seems odd that Marvell was not numbered among the supporters of Buckingham: perhaps he had temporarily been alienated by the Duke's treatment of his wife. All the same there is nothing inherently impossible about Marvell's allegedly favouring James Stuart, whose accession to the throne he seems to have regarded, in March 1677 (see no. 77) with so few misgivings.

BIBLIOGRAPHY: Andrew Browning, *Thomas Osborne*, vol. III, App. 3, pp. 33–44 (Glasgow, 1951).

71 Marvell suspected of belonging to a Dutch fifth-column, 1674.

Public Record Office: SP 105/222, f. 127.

Fugitives.
Mr Carre came to see Us at Rotterdam the $\frac{5}{15}$ May 74. Told Us.
There were certaine young Gentlemen, relations to Parliament men, that had managed all this matter here, during the last session of Parliament.
   They have come over twice or thrice
   Once came over a Parliament man under the name of Mr George by du Moulin's order, was but one night at the Hague, & having spoken with the Prince returned. Carre saw him. was a thicke short man, as Carre judged much like Mervell, but he could not say it was he, though he knows, as he says, Marvell very well.

The above entry made in his diary of government business by Williamson, who was attending the congress at Cologne with Sir Leoline Jenkins, is one of the links in a chain of evidence connecting Marvell with a group of Englishmen who were acting in the Dutch and against the French interest during the Third Dutch War, even before the peace was concluded with Holland in February 1674. Fear of popery had driven Marvell to adopt a position directly opposite to that which he had taken up twenty-one years earlier, with 'The Character of Holland', but the report of the government spy came late enough to absolve him from the possible charge – if not altogether the suspicion – of treasonable activities.

Two further documents of June state that Marvell was going by the alias of 'Mr Thomas', that he had had a quarrel with another member of the group, and, Parliament not sitting, had retired into the country.

72 Engraved portrait of Milton by Faithorne, 1670.

B.M. Department of Prints and Drawings: 1887–10–10–46.

Faithorne's engraving was used as frontispiece to the first edition of Milton's *History of Britain* (1670), where it bears the legend: *Johannis Milton Effigies Aetat. 62. 1670. Gul. Faithorne ad Vivum Delin. et sculpsit.* The original Faithorne portrait in crayons from which the artist himself made the engraving was in the possession of Tonsons, the booksellers, in 1760, when Thomas Hollis employed Cipriani to engrave it.

The precise date and circumstances of Marvell's first acquaintance with Milton are not known for certain, though the terms of the latter's introductory letter of February 1653 (see no. 43) suggest a recent encounter. Marvell's name is prominent in the list drawn up by Edward Phillips of visitors to the blind poet at his house in Petty France between 1652 and 1660, and we know that Marvell sometimes deputised for Milton in his official capacity as Thurloe's Latin secretary (see nos. 58, 61). After the Restoration, when Milton was about to be released from prison, Marvell intervened on his behalf in the House of Commons, and thereafter continued to visit him at his house in Jewin Street.

It was there that he made the acquaintance of Samuel Parker, against whose imputations he defended the older man in the second part of the *Rehearsall Transpros'd* (1673). Shortly before Milton's death he contributed prefatory verses to the second edition of *Paradise Lost* (see no. 73).

BIBLIOGRAPHY: J. Milton French, *Life Records of John Milton*, vol. III, pp.318–19 (New Brunswick, 1954).

73 'On Paradise Lost', before July 1674.
C.124.e.17.

The second edition of Milton's epic poem, entered in the Term Catalogues under the date 6 July 1674, carried commendatory verses in Latin by Samuel Barrow, MD, and in English by Marvell, both sets being signed merely with their writer's initials. Marvell's poem is perhaps one of his last compositions, and it is difficult to accept the condemnation of 'tinkling rhyme' as wholly sincere from one who is not known to have written in any other medium, even despite his amusing exposure of it. Possibly he was glancing at the recent *Transproser Rehears'd*, where Milton is described as a '*Blank Verse* Friend of his, who can by no means endure a Rhyme anywhere but in the Middle of a Verse' (p. 133). Moreover, the verses are marred by a gratuitous attack on Dryden; it is clear enough that Marvell was annoyed by his political time-serving and, perhaps, his public success as a poet. Dryden had sought permission to turn *Paradise Lost* into a rhymed play and, in Aubrey's words, 'Mr. Milton received him civilly, and told him he would give him leave to tagge his verses'. Marvell must have been aware that *The Fall of Angels and man in innocence* had been licensed in April: he refers contemptuously to his former colleague in Cromwell's civil service, in terms of Buckingham's *The Rehearsal*, as 'Town-Bayes', a mere pack-horse poet. Dryden retaliated in the preface to *Religio Laici* (1682) with a reference to '*Martin Mar-Prelate* (the *Marvel* of those times) . . . the first Presbyterian Scribler who sanctify'd Libels and Scurrility to the use of the Good Old Cause'.

Engraved portrait of Milton by Faithorne, 1670 (72)

74 'Andrew Marvell's Cottage' at Highgate, about 1860.
B.M. Department of Prints and Drawings: Potter Collection VII, p. 112.

Marvell's connection with Highgate admits of little doubt. Writing to Sir Edward Harley on 3 May 1673 he remarks that 'I intend by the end of the next week to betake my selfe some five miles of to injoy the spring & my privacy', and a letter written to Trinity House on 24 June is dated from Highgate. In June or July 1675 he resolves 'to sequester [him] self one whole Day' there in order to answer a letter from William Popple.

The Potter Collection also includes a cutting from the *North Middlesex Chronicle* for 25 March 1882, reporting a lecture on Marvell given by John Taylor of the British Museum at

'Andrew Marvell's Cottage' at Highgate, about 1860 (74)

the Highgate Literary and Scientific Institution four days previously. During the lecture Taylor 'read several hitherto unpublished letters written by Marvell to his friends and dated from High Gate'. These are now seemingly unknown.

The house in this photograph is that which tradition, dating back at least to the middle of last century, associates with the poet. It stood next to Lauderdale House and was pulled down in 1869 to make way for Sir Sidney Waterlow's house and garden, now part of Waterlow Park. The house is perhaps rather larger than would have been necessary for a bachelor, even with the single horse and man that Parker slightingly allowed him, being assessed at seven hearths in the Hearth Tax Rolls of 1662–75, when it was occupied by George Pryor, a merchant of London. On Pryor's death shortly afterwards it passed to his daughter Mary, the wife of Charles Izard, who lived there until 1681.

BIBLIOGRAPHY: Percy W. Lovell and William McB. Marcham, *The Village of Highgate* (*Survey of London*, vol. XVII), 1936, pp. 16–17.

75 Engraved portrait of Thomas Osborne when Earl of Danby, by Abraham Blooteling, after Lely, about 1674.
B.M. Department of Prints and Drawings: 1870-7-9-292

Osborne (1632–1712), who later became Duke of Leeds, was Lord Treasurer from June 1673, that is, shortly before the publication of *The Rehearsall Transpros'd*, Part II, until seven months after Marvell's death, and the anecdote first related by Cooke, if not apocryphal, must therefore belong to this period.

. . . Mr. *Marvell*, who then lodged up two Pair of Stairs in a little Court in the *Strand*, was writing when the Lord Treasurer opened the Door abruptly upon him. Surprized at the Sight of so unexpected a Visiter, he told him he believed he had mistook his Way. The Lord *Danby* replyed, not now I have found Mr. *Marvell*, telling him that he came with a Message from his Majesty, which was to know what he could do to serve him. His Answer was, in his usual facetious Manner, that it was not in his Majesty's Power to serve him. But coming to a serious Explanation of his Meaning, he told the Lord Treasurer he knew the Nature of Courts full well, he had been in many; that whoever is distinguished by a Prince's Favours is certainly expected to vote in his Interest. The Lord *Danby* told him, his Majesty had only a just Sense of his Merits, in Regard to which alone he desired to know whether there was any Place at Court he could be pleased with. These Offers had no Effect on him, tho urged with the greatest Earnestness. He told the Lord Treasurer he could not accept them with Honour, for he must be either ingrateful to the King in voting against him, or false to his Country in giving into the Measures of the Court; therefore the only Favour he beged of his Majesty was, that he would esteem him as dutyful a Subject as any he had, and more in his proper Interest in refusing his Offers, than if he had embraced them. The Lord *Danby*, finding no Arguments could prevail, told him the King his Master had ordered a thousand Pounds for him, which he hoped he would receive, till he could think what farther to ask of his Majesty. This last Offer was rejected with the same Stedfastness of Mind, as was the first; tho, as soon as the Lord Treasurer was gone, he was forced to send to a Friend to borrow a Guinea . . .

76 Payment of Marvell's stipend as Member of Parliament for Hull, 18 October 1675.

Hull City Archives: BRF/3/25.

The entry in the corporation cash book relating to the thirteenth session of the Cavalier, or by now the Pensionary, Parliament (13 April–9 June 1675) reads in part: 'By C[ouncil] to Mr Danl. Hoare to remit to Coll^o Antho: Gilby & Andrew Marvell Esqr for 59. days each of them appeared for the Town in Parliament last Session at 6shs 8^d per day – each man's part is 19^l 13shs 4^d.'

The origin of parliamentary wages can be traced back to the 'Knight's pence' of the Middle Ages. Payment of them was made, and required, less and less frequently under the Tudors and early Stuarts until the time of the Long Parliament, whose sessions brought heavy expenses upon its members: after the Restoration, when the country gentry began to recapture the urban seats, the custom decayed once more. Parker sneeringly remarked that it had 'a long time been antiquated and out of date, Gentlemen despising so vile a stipend, that was

Engraved portrait of
Thomas Osborne by Abraham Blooteling,
about 1674 (75)

given like alms to the poor yet [Marvell] requir'd it for the sake of a bare subsistance, altho' in this mean poverty he was nevertheless haughty and insolent.'

It is true that we do not know what other means of support Marvell had, though he was apparently not without substance at his death (see no. 113). Aubrey calls Marvell's 'an honourable pension', and it may have been Parker who was indirectly responsible for the often-repeated but wholly erroneous assertion that he was the last man to receive such payment.

BIBLIOGRAPHY: R. C. Latham, 'Payment of Parliamentary wages – the last phase', *English Historical Review*, LXVI (1951), 27–50.

77 Marvell's speech in the House, 27 March 1677.

Egerton MS 3345, f.41.

Osborne, now Earl of Danby and leader of the ruling Court Party, hoped to conciliate Protestant prejudice by proposing securities against the possible abuse of ecclesiastical patronage by a Roman Catholic ruler. He introduced in the Lords a bill that required the declaration against transubstantiation to be extended to future sovereigns who, if they refused, were to forfeit the exclusive right of appointment to bishoprics and benefices, which would be presided over instead by a committee of the clergy. Marvell, who on 6 March 1675 had been appointed a commissioner for recusancy in Yorkshire and who might be expected to object on the grounds both that this implied a Catholic might rule and that it gave excessive powers to the clergy, was surprisingly bland, observing at its second reading 'That the King being in health, and the hearts of Princes in the almighty he might turne them before they came to the Crowne, and [he was] against goeing about to prevent things att soe great a distance, as this seemed to bee'.

On the same day he was appointed to the committee that sat upon this and a bill 'to hinder Papists from sitting in either House of Parliament'. Although the committee returned the bill with suitable amendments three days later sudden developments in foreign affairs diverted attention and it was allowed to drop.

78 Map-view of west-central London, engraved by Hollar, about 1658–66.

B.M. Department of Prints and Drawings: Hollar VIII, 38.

The earliest indication that Marvell lived in Covent Garden occurs in a letter of John Fisher, an attorney in the exchequer, of 9 January 1677, which is addressed to him 'at his Lodgings at Mr James Shawes house in Maiden Lane'. This house formerly stood on the south side of Maiden Lane, on the site of the present no. 9, where is now the Vaudeville Theatre.

After directing Mary Palmer, about June of that year, to take a house in Great Russell Street for the concealment of the bankrupts Nelthorpe and Thompson, Marvell maintained this lodging 'for his privacy . . . where he kept his money bonds bills Jewells writeings & other goods & chattles'. Caution demanded that it remain his official address, and we find him dating letters thence between December 1677 and the following April: it may perhaps be the lodging described by Cooke in the famous anecdote (see no. 75). During the illness that overtook him on his return from Hull in August 1678, however, he naturally lay in the Great Russell Street house, where he could be nursed by Mary Palmer, and on his death was therefore buried in the church which served that parish, rather than in St Paul's, Covent Garden.

Hollar's superb view, which is an incomplete sheet of an intended large-scale map, shows street lines in plan and buildings in isometric projection. It may well give a generally accurate impression of the area covered, but if it was executed during the Interregnum, its details must be treated with some caution, since not until after 1670 was the north side of Maiden Lane built up in the manner indicated.

79 Marvell's letter to Sir Edward Harley, 7 August 1677.

Portland Papers: B.L. Loan 29/182, f.249.

When, in February 1677, Parliament met after a prorogation of fifteen months, the Duke of Buckingham raised the question of its legality, invoking two unrepealed statutes of Edward III. The Earls of Shaftesbury and Salisbury, with Lord Wharton, supported his notion and, on refusing to submit, all four were committed to the Tower. Shaftesbury alone was not released until the following February, but the others had procured their liberty by the date of Marvell's letter.

Marvell's statements about Buckingham's freedom being obtained by 'Nelly, Midlesex, Rochester, and the merry gang', and his living 'in Whitehall at my L: Rochester's logings leading the usuall life', sound perhaps more ominous than was the case. Since January 1674, when the Lords called him to account for his scandalous

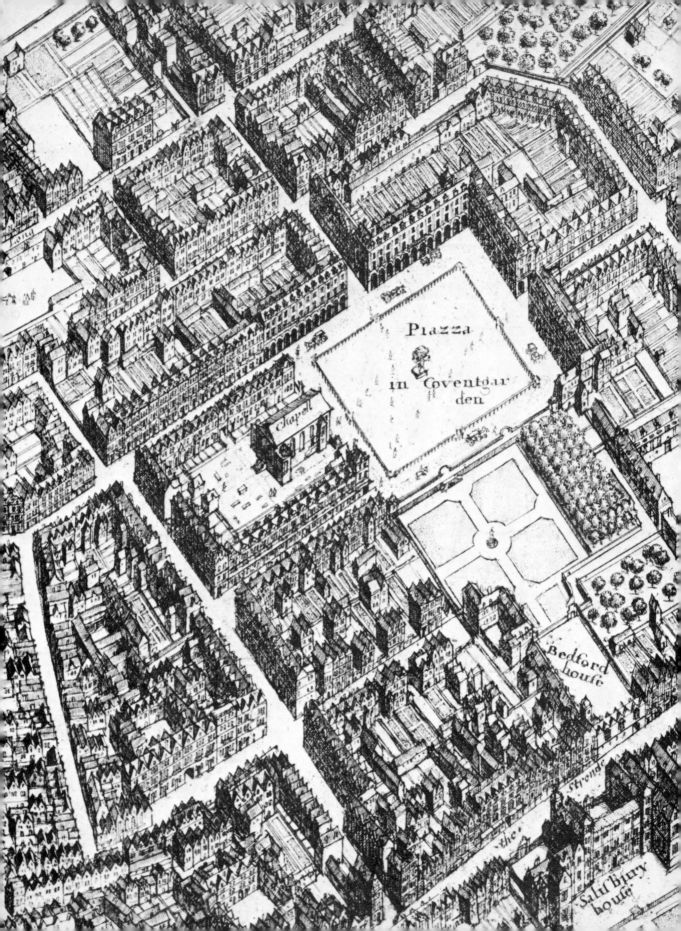

Address of Marvell's letter to Hull Trinity House, 25 February 1678 (81)

conduct with the Countess of Coventry, the husband of Marvell's former pupil had largely reformed himself. As Marvell observed elsewhere, 'he was so far a Gainer, that with the loss of his Offices, and dependence, he was restored to the Freedom of his own Spirit, to give thence-forward those admirable Proofs of the Vigour, and Vivacity of his better Judgement, in Asserting, though to his own Imprisonment, the due Liberties of the *English* Nation' (*Account of the Growth of Popery*).

Marvell's correspondent, a Presbyterian and former officer in the Parliamentary forces, but subsequently an opponent of Cromwell, was at the Restoration appointed Governor of Dunkirk, but was given an honourable discharge when he opposed the sale of the town. In the Cavalier Parliament he belonged to the Country Party and was an opponent of legislation against non-conformists. There was thus sufficient reason why, by 1673, he should be drawn into friendship with the poet.

80 Engraved portrait of Philip, fourth Baron Wharton, by Hollar.

B.M. Department of Prints and Drawings: Parthey 1323.

Lord Wharton (1613–96) joined the Parliamentary army at the outbreak of the Civil War, earning at Edgehill the sobriquet, possibly undeserved, of 'sawpit Wharton', after his alleged place of refuge. Though thereafter he confined himself to purely parliamentary duties, he was on very intimate terms with Cromwell, with whose family he contemplated an alliance in 1652. However, he declined to sit in Cromwell's House of Lords in 1657, and at the Restoration suffered only the loss of some lands acquired under the Commonwealth.

In religious matters Wharton favoured the non-conformists, and in 1676 is recorded (Egerton MS 3330, ff. 14, 16) as a regular attender at a meeting-house in Covent Garden, not far from Marvell's lodgings there. In the winter of 1671/2 Marvell was his guest at Winchendon,

Buckinghamshire, whence he corresponded
with Dr Benjamin Worsley about a proposed
match for one of Wharton's sons.

It was to Wharton that, in a letter dated 2
April 1667, Marvell communicated one of his
very few surviving specimens of literary criti-
cism, concerning parallel English and Latin
versions of a poem by Simon Ford, published
as *The Conflagration of London: practically de-
lineated . . . :* 'The Latin . . . (if I may presume
to censure in your Lordships presence) hath
severall excellent heights, but the English translation is not so good; and both of them strain for
wit and conceit more then becomes the gravity
of the author or the sadnesse of the subject.' As,
in Aubrey's phrase, 'an excellent poet in Latin
or English', Marvell may be supposed a good
judge in these matters.

81 Marvell's letter to Trinity House, Hull, 25 February 1678.
The Warden and the Corporation of the Hull Trinity House.

Marvell's connection with the Hull Seaman's
Guild, generally known from the Middle Ages
as Trinity House, began after his second return
to Parliament for the town, in the year that
Charles II confirmed and more clearly defined
the charters that his predecessors had granted in
1541 and 1581. The services that he, with his
fellow Member for Hull, was able to perform for
the institution are witnessed in the present letter
by the 'Token', that is gift, sent to him by the
Wardens: Margoliouth records presents of
money and ale, together with 'treats' on his
visits to Hull.

Three out of every four of the sixty-nine
letters extant from Marvell to Trinity House,
however, concern negotiations for the building
of a lighthouse at Spurn Head, which by the
time of Marvell's death was still not brought
to a successful conclusion. Moreover, unlike
Anthony Gilby he never became one of the
Honorary Brethren, though three months after
the date of the present letter he was elected a
Younger Warden of the sister house at London.

The seal that Marvell used on his letters to
Trinity House bore, appropriately enough, a
ship (see no. 83E).

Engraved portrait of
Philip, 4th Baron Wharton,
by Hollar (80)

his father was Minister of - - - - - - - - - -   he was
borne. He had good Grammar-education; and after sent to - -
- - - - - - - in Cambridge. . In the time of Oliver
the Protector he was Latin Secretarie. He was a great master
of the Latin tongue: an excellent poet in Latin or English:
for Latin verses there was no man would come into compe-
-tition with him. The verses called the advice to the Pain-
-ter were of his making. His native towne of Hull loved
him so well that they elected him for their representative in Parli-
-ament, and gave him an honourable pension to maintaine him.
He was of a middling stature, pretty strong sett, roundish faced,
cherry cheekt, hazell eie, browne haire; he was in his conversation very modest & of very
few words. Though he loved wine he would never drinke hard
in company: and was wont to say, that he would not play the
good-fellow in any mans company, in whose hands he would not
trust his life. He kept bottles of wine at his lodgeings, and
many times he would drinke liberally by himselfe: to refresh
his spirits, and exalt his Muse. I remember I have been told
by the learned . . . . [an high German] was wont to keep
bottells of good Rhenish-wine in his studie, and when he had
spent his spirits, he would drinke a good Rummer of it.
James Harrington Esq. was his intimate friend. J. Pell D. D. was
one of his acquaintance. He had not a general acquaintance.
He wrote The Rehersall transprosed. , Mr Smirke. [stitcht
4to about 8 sheets] The naked Truth.

Obijt Londini Aug. 18. 1678, and is buryed in St Giles church
in the fields, about the middle of the south aisle. Some suspect
that he was poysoned by the Jesuites, but I cannot be positive.
I remember I heard him say that the Earle of Rochester was the
only man in England that had the true veine of Satyre.

     He was wont to say, that he would not drinke high or
freely with any one with whom he would not intrust his Life.

     He lies interred under the Pewes in the south side of Saint
Giles church in the fields under the window wherein is painted in
glasse a Red-Lyon [it was given by the Innekeeper of the red
Lyon Inne in Holborne] and is the . . . . window from the east.
This account I had from the Sexton, that made his grave.

82 John Aubrey's account of Marvell, after February 1680.

Bodleian Aubrey MS 6, f.104.

He was of a middling stature, pretty strong sett, roundish faced, cherry cheek't, hazell eie, browne haire; he was in his conversation very modest and of very few words. Though he loved wine he would never drinke hard in company: and was wont to say, *that he would not play the good-fellow in any mans company in whose hands he would not trust his life.* He kept bottles of wine at his lodgeing, and many times he would drinke liberally by himself: to refresh his spirits, and exalt his Muse . . . James Harrington Esq was his intimate friend. J[ohn] Pell D. D. was one of his acquaintance. He had not a generall acquaintance . . .

Although Aubrey (1626–97) may have encountered Marvell during his own early days as a student at the Middle Temple between 1646 and 1656, or at the meetings of the Rota club in the winter of 1659–60 that he attended as auditor, the details given in his notes and elsewhere suggest that his recollections were of the poet in his fifties. Marvell's statement that Rochester 'was the only man in England that had the true veine of Satyre' could scarcely have been elicited by anything that he wrote before 1675 or 1676. We may also consider Marvell's promise to Aubrey to write the life of Milton, who died in November 1674 – for which space was left in the present manuscript, on the page facing Marvell's own life – and the observation that he had 'made a good epitaph' for James Harrington, who died in September 1677.

The manuscript itself is dated on its first page 'Febr. 24. 1679/80'. Aubrey made several attempts at recording Marvell's dictum, quoted above, and his final version, which no editor seems to have noted, runs as follows: 'He was wont to say, that he would not drinke high or freely with any one with whom he would not intrust his Life'.

The final paragraph in the manuscript account (see no.110) was added by Anthony Wood whose notes on Marvell, published in *Athenae Oxonienses* (1691-2), are based on Aubrey, but include fuller bibliographical details.

83 Seals used by Marvell during the period 1659–78.

Some half-a-dozen seals are found on letters written to various correspondents by Marvell throughout his career as member of Parliament for Hull. They are all probably impressions from signet rings, with the exception of D below, and are as follows.

A: The earliest seal known to have been used by Marvell – since the one with which he sealed the Hull deed of November 1647 is missing – shows the head of a Caesar facing the observer's left, within an oval rim measuring at its widest points approximately 18 × 14 cm. It occurs on several letters written between February 1659 and April 1669 (Misc. Letter 5 and Hull Corporation Letter 99 in the Oxford edition), and may have been discarded entirely in favour of the first stag seal. Add. MS 22919, f.79b.

B: Marvell's stag seal, which was in use between about November 1669 and December 1677 (Hull Corporation Letter 104 and Misc. Letter 42: in Grosart's day it appeared also on Hull Corporation Letter 246), represents the beast looking towards the observer's right, within a roughly circular rim measuring approximately 12 cm in diameter. It is not known whether the stag had any particular significance for Marvell: it does not figure in his arms or as his crest. Reproduced from B.L. (Portland) Loan 29/182.

C: A second stag seal, which is found in his letter to Harley of 30 June 1677 (Misc. Letter 40), is somewhat cruder in execution than the other, which it closely resembles in size. The beast is facing the observer's left and over its back appear the letters I T S, probably signifying a motto such as 'In Te[Domine] Speravi'. Reproduced from B.L. (Portland) Loan 29/80, art. 20.

D: The seal used by Marvell on his letter to Harley of 1 July 1676 (Misc. Letter 35) is a fine armorial one measuring approximately 18 cm in diameter and having a shield of four quarterings. While the first and third quarters bear some resemblance to Marvell's arms (see p. 114), the whole coat is credibly that of a member of the Farrington family, as recorded in Burke's *General Armory* (1884) and in the Harleian Society's *Visitation of London* (1880, vol. xv). It may, therefore, indicate an earlier connection

with the merchant John Farrington than has hitherto been suspected. Reproduced from B.L. (Portland) Loan 29/80, art. 20.

E: Marvell's letter to Trinity House, Hull, of 25 February 1678 (no 51 in the published series) is sealed with a ship, sailing towards the observer's left, within a circular rim.

F: Marvell's letter to Hull Corporation of 12 March 1663 (no. 31 in Margoliouth's edition) bears the poor and damaged impression of what may be a scorpion seal. The letter was written from Vianen in the Netherlands and it is possible that the seal was a borrowed one.

Satirist in Verse

The Painter so, long having vext his cloth,
Of his Hound's Mouth to feign the raging froth,
His desperate Pencil at the work did dart,
His Anger reacht that rage which past his Art;
Chance finisht that which Art could but begin,
And he sat smiling how his Dog did grinn.
So may'st thou perfect, by a lucky blow,
What all thy softest touches cannot do.
                    'The last Instructions to a Painter', ll. 21–8

WITH the exception of 'The last Instructions to a Painter', considerable doubts have been expressed regarding the authenticity of the dozen and a half or so verse-satires that have at various times been attributed to Marvell, nor is the debate likely ever to reach a definitive conclusion. The writer of virulent political satire in verse does not normally advertise his authorship; naturally enough no manuscripts in Marvell's autograph are known, and but for the disputed additions made to the Bodleian copy of *Miscellaneous Poems* no witnesses of comparable authority have been discovered. Moreover, the style offers no very reliable guide in a medium that is so far removed from lyric or other occasional verse, while the views expressed in the satires, though compatible with Marvell's are not, of course, exclusively his property.

When all this has been said, however, it supplies no conclusive evidence against Marvell's authorship: probabilities may be taken into account even if they seem unlikely ever to become certainties, and the area that must include the true canon is relatively small and well-defined. The pieces normally claimed as his are datable to the period 1667–77; they begin, that is, with Marvell's first serious involvement in a major political issue and reflect a disillusion with the monarchy and a hatred of authoritarianism, both political and religious, that chimes with what is otherwise known of his development over these years. It has, however, recently been suggested that two slightly earlier satires also belong to the canon.

The satires among which Marvell's work is to be sought are largely comprised in Bodleian MS Eng. poet. d. 49. In order of copying here, which reflects fairly accurately the sequence of composition, they run as follows: the Second and Third Advices (dated here to April and 1 October 1666), 'Clarindon's House-Warming' (about July 1667), 'The Last Instructions to a Painter' (dated to 4 September 1667), 'The King's Vows' (May 1670), 'The Loyall Scot' (between 1667 and 1673), *Bludius et Corona* and its English counterpart (after 9 May 1671), 'Upon the cutting Sir John Coventry's Nose' (after 21 December 1670), 'The Statue in Stocks Market' (about 1672–5), 'Upon His Majesty's being made Free of the City' (after 18 December 1674), 'The Statue at Charing Cross' (July 1675), 'The Chequer Inn' (April 1675) and *Scaevola Scoto-Britannus* (after 24 January

1677). Of the remaining two satires presumably thought to be Marvell's by the compiler only 'The Doctor turn'd Justice' (about 1672) was written during his lifetime. It will be remarked that the only notable omission in this list among the satires conjecturally attributed to Marvell by various modern editors is 'Further Advice to a Painter' (1670–1).

84 Engraved portrait of Edward Hyde, first Earl of Clarendon, by David Loggan.

B.M. Department of Prints and Drawings: Cracherode P5–253.

Edward Hyde (1609–74) was before the Civil War a successful barrister who took part in organising the impeachment of Strafford. Having withdrawn from the popular party, however, his abilities attracted the notice of the King whose close adviser he became at York and at Oxford, a trust which, despite opposition from Henrietta Maria, he held with the new king during his exile in France.

As Lord Chancellor and Earl of Clarendon after the Restoration he was anxious to re-establish episcopacy in England and Scotland, though it was to have been, until rejected by a solidly Anglican House of Commons, a limited episcopacy, with revision of the Prayer Book and concessions in ritual. Nor did he favour the inflexible operation of the Act of Uniformity, but when his attempts at comprehension failed he thought it his duty to support the law. He opposed the King's first Declaration of Indulgence in 1662, and in the following year was faced with an unsuccessful impeachment for high treason.

His final misfortune was to become involved in the First and Second Dutch Wars, and contrary to popular prejudice he denied having any major share in the sale of Dunkirk. After the humiliation at Chatham, he was deprived of office by the King, who remarked that 'his behaviour and humour was grown so unsupportable to myself and to all the world else, that I could no longer endure it'; the articles of his impeachment were drawn up in October 1667. Before he could be brought to his trial he fled to France, where he was compelled to spend the rest of his life and where he compiled and revised his *History of the Rebellion*.

85 'Clarindon's House-Warming', about June or July 1667.

Bodleian Douce MS 357, ff.155b, 156.

The composition of 'Clarindon's House-Warming' falls between 25 June and 25 July 1667, the dates on which Parliament was summoned and actually met. Its occasion was the completion of Clarendon House in the previous spring, which had cost the Chancellor fifty thousand pounds – three times the original estimate. Clarendon had thought that the employment thus provided during the year of the plague and the Great Fire would have been welcomed, but he found the expense resented and the house nicknamed Dunkirk House in allusion to the sale of that town to the French which was popularly supposed to have financed the building.

> The *Scotch* Forts & *Dunkirk*, but that they were sold,
> He would have demolisht to raise up his Walls;
> Nay ev'n from *Tangier* have sent back for the mold,
> But that he had nearer the Stones of St. *Pauls*.

This boisterous satire on Lord Chancellor Clarendon and his new house in Piccadilly was first printed in *Directions to a Painter . . . being the Last Works of Sir John Denham. Whereunto is annexed, Clarindon's House-Warming. By an Unknown Author*', 1667. A copy of the work in Bodleian Gough MS London 14 incorporates important contemporary manuscript corrections to 'Clarindon's House-Warming', which was first printed as Marvell's by Thomas Cooke in 1726, along with an epigram 'Upon his House', from the *State Poems* of 1697; Grosart added a distich 'Upon his Grand-Children'.

86 'The Last Instructions to a Painter', about September 1667.

993.l.43(1).

The genre of Advice-to-a-Painter poems to which Marvell's longest satire belongs came into England from Italy: Waller was the first original artist to naturalise it, in a wholly serious panegyric of the Duke of York's conduct during the First Dutch War in 1665. The form, however, was taken over in the following year for two satires, generally referred to as the First and Second Advices, which were printed in 1667, together with a Fourth and Fifth, in a volume entitled *Directions to a Painter . . . Being the Last Works of Sir John Denham*. The attribution is false; but since the volume concluded with Marvell's 'Clarindon's House-Warming' (see no. 85), most of the Advices have at one time or another been claimed for him. His Oxford editor remarked of 'The last Instructions' that 'of all the satires attributed to Marvell there is none of which one can feel less doubt'. Like the other Advices it is directed in part against the (by then former) Lord Chancellor, Clarendon, but principally against the corruptions of government that made possible the humiliating victory of De Ruyter in the Medway.

The satire was composed, as is evident from internal factors, between 30 August and 26 October 1667: the manuscript copy in Bodleian MS Eng. poet. d. 49 bears the date '4 September' after the title, probably with reason, and Osborne MS PB VII/15 is similarly dated to that month. The poem is shown here in its earliest printed text, that of *The Third Part of the Collection of Poems on Affairs of State*, 1689.

87 'The Last Instructions to a Painter'.

Add. MS 18220, f.23.

Marvell's satire opens with a libellous attack on three members of the Court, all of whom are arraigned for licentiousness. By comparison with his treatment of the Duchess of York and the Countess of Castlemaine, Marvell's bawdy insinuations against Henry Jermyn are mild enough. Jermyn, created Earl of St Albans at the Restoration, had during the years of exile acted

Extract from 'The Last Instructions to a Painter' (87)

as Henrietta Maria's secretary at the Louvre. As Charles II's ambassador to the French Court he maintained a close contact with her, and it was under cover of attending to her affairs that he was employed by Clarendon in January 1667 secretly to negotiate the treaty of Breda with the Dutch.

The present extract, entitled 'A Libell Taken out of the Painter, upon H. Jermyn E of St Albans', was communicated on 10 July 1668 by Henry North, son of Sir Henry, MP for Suffolk, to the Reverend John Watson, vicar of Mildenhall, who copied it into the commonplace-book of verse that he had begun about 1667.

Medallion showing the
Dutch victory in the Medway
by Pieter van Abeele (89)

88 'The Last Instructions'.
Osborn MS PB VII/15.

The central section of this satire describes the advance up the Medway, on 10 June 1667, of the Dutch fleet under De Ruyter, guided by a disaffected English pilot, their breaking the chain at Chatham, burning the idle and deserted English vessels and capturing the *Royal Charles* – all of which was accomplished with scarcely a show of opposition, except by Captain Douglas. De Ruyter's entry into the estuary is described (ll. 523–50) in terms almost of a summer regatta, concluding with a disarming simile:

> So have I seen in Aprill's Bud, arise
> A fleet of Clouds, sayling along the skyes,
> The liquid Region with their Squadrons fill'd,
> Their Ayery Sternes the Sun behind does guild;
> And gentle Gales them Steere, & Heaven drives,
> When all on suddain their cold bosome rives
> With Thunder & Lightning from each armed Cloud,
> Shepherds in vaine themselves in Bushes shrowde.
> So up the Stream the Belgick Navy glides,
> And at Sheernesse unloades its stormy sides.

89 Medallion commemorating the Dutch victory in the Medway, 10 June 1667.
B.M. Department of Coins and Medals: M.I., 1, 533/182.

The scene shown here was executed by the celebrated Dutch medallist Pieter van Abeele, who worked at Amsterdam between 1622 and his death in 1677. It illustrates the burning of the English fleet by De Ruyter at Chatham, and the shell beneath bears an inscription in Dutch which may be translated: 'June 1667. By order of their High Mightinesses, and under the command of Sir Michael, son of Adrien de Ruyter, Lieutenant-Admiral-General, the ships of war of the King were attacked, burnt and sunk in the river of Chatham.'

The reverse, which is the work of the same craftsman, commemorates the Treaty of Breda.

90 'The Loyall Scot', about 1667–73.
Sloane MS 655, f.18.

In June 1667 the Dutch fleet under De Ruyter sailed up the Medway, on their return burning

Opening line
'The Loyall Scot' (

The Loyall Scot

upon occasion of the death of Capt Douglas
Burnt in one of his Ma.ies shipps at Chatham

By Cleaveland's Ghost

When the old Heroes of the warlike shades
Saw Douglas walkeing on the Elizian glades
They streight consulted gathering in a Ring
Which of theire Poets should his welcome sing
And as a fauourable pennance chose
Cleaueland on whome they would the task impose
Hee vnderstood and willingly addrest
His ready muse to court the warlike Guest
Much had hee cured the humour of his vein
Hee judg'd more clearly now and saw more plaine
For those soft aires had temper'd euery thought
And of wise Lethe hee had tooke a draught
Abruptly hee began (disguising Art)
As of his Satyr this had been a part)
Not Joe deare Douglas on whose louely Chin
The early downe but newly did begin
And modest beauty still his Sex did veil
While Envious virgins hope hee is a male
His shady locks curle back themselues to seeke
No other courtshipp knew but to his cheeke
Oft as hee in chill Esk or Seine by night
Hardend and cool'd those limbs so soft so white
Amongst the reeds to be espy'd by him
The Nymphs would rush and he would forward swim
They sighed and said fond boy why soe vntame
That flyes loues fires reserue for other flame
Fixt on his shipp he fought the horrid day
And wondred much at those whoe ran away
Noe other feare himselfe could comprehend
Then least Heauen fall ere thither he assend
With Birding at the Dutch as if in sport
He enterteins the while his time too short

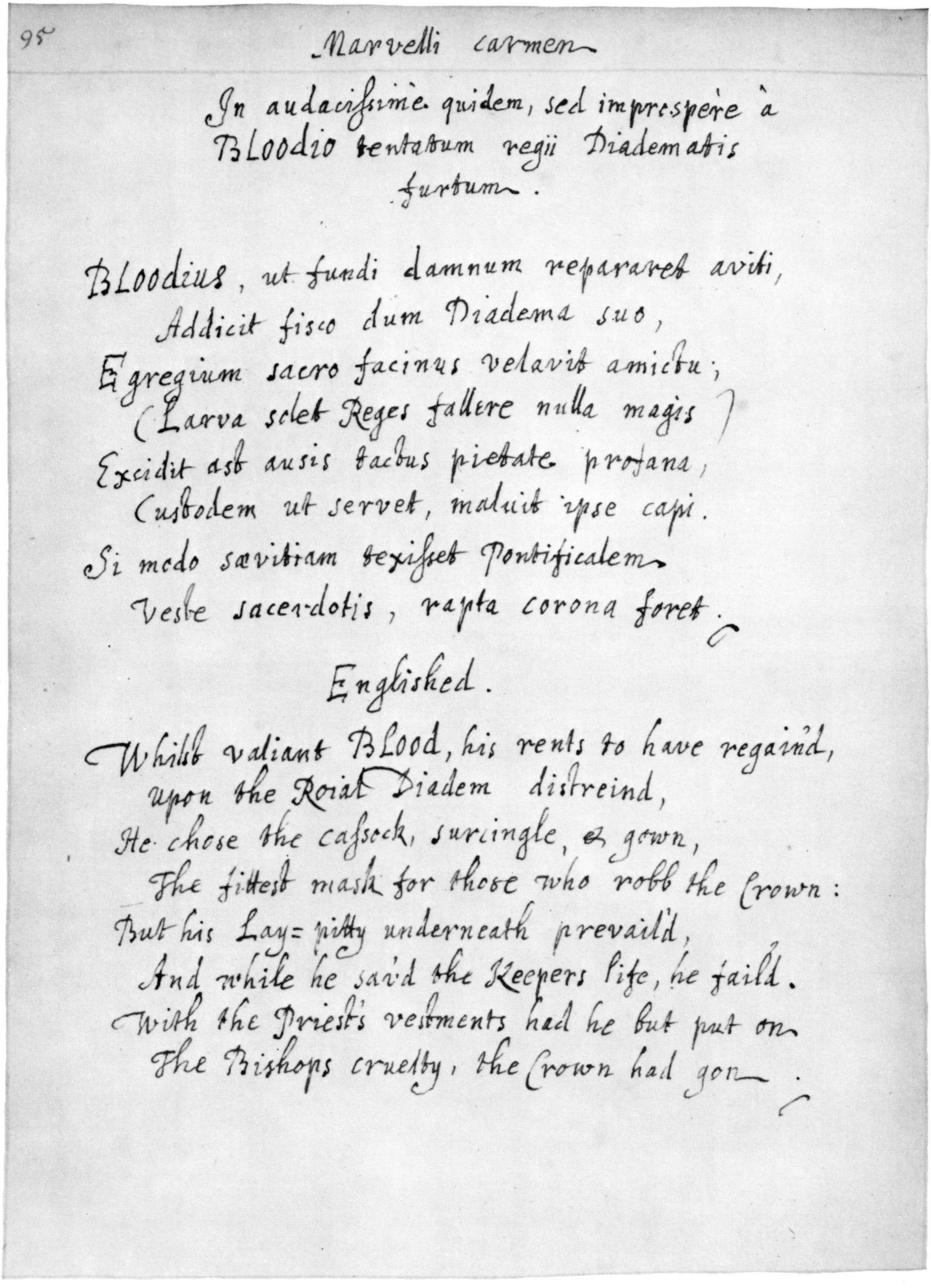

95

Marvelli carmen.

In audacissimè quidem, sed improsperè à
Bloodio tentatum regii Diadematis
furtum.

Bloodius, ut fundi damnum repararet aviti,
  Addicit fisco dum Diadema suo,
Egregium sacro facinus velavit amictu;
  (Larva solet Reges fallere nulla magis)
Excidit ast ausis tactus pietate profana,
  Custodem ut servet, maluit ipse capi.
Si modo sævitiam texisset Pontificalem
  Veste sacerdotis, rapta corona foret.

Englished.

Whilst valiant BLOOD, his rents to have regain'd,
  upon the Roial Diadem distreind,
He chose the cassock, surcingle, & gown,
  The fittest mask for those who robb the Crown:
But his Lay=pitty underneath prevaild,
  And while he savd the Keepers life, he faild.
With the Priest's vestments had he but put on
The Bishops cruelty, the Crown had gon.

The Blood epigrams (91)

The Royal Oak 'and in her captain *Douglass*, . . . [who] . . . had received orders to defend his ship, which he did with the utmost resolution; but, having none to retire, he chose to burn with her, rather than live to be reproached with having deserted his command'. Despite the implication of this extract from Campbell's *Lives of the Admirals* (1750), Archibald Douglas was not a naval captain but commanded a company of Lord George Douglas's Scottish regiment that had been recalled from service against the French.

The nucleus of Marvell's poem is the description (in ll. 15–62) of Douglas's death, which originally formed part of 'The last Instructions' and was therefore written in 1667. The opening and concluding verses (ll. 274–85) form the framework, in which the satirist John Cleveland, author in 1643 of 'The Rebell Scot', is made to greet Douglas in the Elysian Fields, while a further passage asserts the essential unity of England and Scotland: these lines were probably composed in 1669–70 when a parliamentary union was in question. Inserted in the middle of this passage on unity is a fiercely abusive tirade (ll. 87–253) against the alleged chief opponents of union, the bishops, which also incorporates the English version of *Bludius et Corona*, and was probably written about 1672–3. The authorship of this section has been much disputed: it appears, however, in three contemporary manuscript copies of the poem, of which the present manuscript is one.

91 *Bludius et Corona*, after 9 May 1671.
Sloane MS 3413, f.29b.

The nucleus of this poem, which survives in parallel Latin and English versions, is given in Marvell's letter to a friend in Persia of 9 August 1671:

One *Blud*, outlawed for a Plot to take *Dublin* Castle, and who seized on the *Duke of Ormond* here last Year, and might have killed him, a most bold, and yet sober, Fellow, some Months ago seized the Crown and Sceptre in the Tower, took them away, and, if he had killed the Keeper, might have carryed them clear off. He, being taken, astonished the King and Court, with the Generosity, and Wisdom, of his Answers. He, and all his Accomplices, for his Sake, are discharged by the King, to the Wonder of all.

An informer's report to Joseph Williamson, dated 21 September 1671, connects Blood with Marvell as agents of the Duke of Buckingham, Ormonde's greatest opponent.

The English version of *Bludius et Corona* had certainly been composed by the following 5 August, when it was entered in the commonplace collection that is now Add. MS 18220 (see no. 87). The present copy, which provides independent testimony to Marvell's authorship, was copied into his notebook by Dr Walter Charleton (1619–1707), Charles II's physician and a High Churchman, who was also a friend of Aubrey. The transcriber of another manuscript (Bodleian Douce MS 357) assumes the English to have been the earlier version: we may consider, however, that a similar satire on the 'Bishops' cruelty', *Scaevola Scoto-Britannus*, written after January 1677, is not known to exist at all in English. The priority of Marvell's parallel versions is always difficult, if not impossible, to estimate, but what matters more for the sake of his reputation is the skill that makes them so.

92 'Upon His Majesty's being made Free of the City', about December 1674.
Harley MS 7315, ff.52b,53.

After Charles II had done Sir Robert Viner the honour of attending his installation as Lord Mayor of London in October 1674, the grateful aldermen went on 18 December to Whitehall '& presented the King his Freedome in a golden box of 1000^{li} value. They will afterwards proportionally to the Duke [of York] . . .' (Miscellaneous Letter 28).

In this satire, which is couched in the doggerel stanza commonly employed for the songs sung at the Lord Mayor's table during the annual festivities, the Common Council of London's grave and industrious citizens and merchants are taken to task for admitting to the freedom of their City the wastrel King, who is portrayed as the archetypal idle apprentice.

He spends all his Days
In running to Plays,
When in his Shop, he shou'd be poreing
And wasts all his Nights
In his constant Delights
Of Revelling, Drinking, & Whoreing.

The text shown here is from an important manuscript collection of satires of the reign of Charles II, that bears on its first page the purchase date of 25 March 1703. It includes several pieces commonly attributed to Marvell and Rochester.

93 'The Statue in Stocks Market', about 1672–5.
93.h.1.

In May 1672 Sir Robert Viner, a wealthy goldsmith of London, presented to Charles II the equestrian statue of the monarch that he had erected at his own charge in Stocks Market, on the site of the present Mansion House. Margoliouth observed that this satire seems to have been written not for the presentation, but when the statue had been covered up for alterations, and suggested a *prima facie* case for 1675, the year of 'The Statue at Charing Cross'.

The statue is now at Newby Hall, Ripon. Two years before its removal from Stocks Market in 1736 James Ralph published, in *A Critical Review of the Publick Buildings . . . in . . . London*, the following somewhat inaccurate account of it, that provides the background to the satire.

This statue was originally made for *John Sobieski*, King of *Poland*, but, by some accident, was left upon the workman's hands: about the same time, the city was loyal enough to pay their devoirs to King *Charles*, immediately upon his restoration; and, finding this statue ready made to their hands, resolv'd to do it the cheapest way, and convert the *Polander* into a *Briton*, and the *Turk*, underneath his horse, into *Oliver Cromwell*, to make their compliment compleat.

The satire is shown here as it was printed in Thompson's edition of 1776 (vol.1, pp.viii, ix) from 'a volume of Mr. Marvell's poems, some written with his own hand, and the rest copied by his order' that had been given to him by Thomas Raikes, but is now unknown.

94 'The Statue at Charing Cross', 1675.
11609.cc.28.

The erection of the bronze equestrian statue of Charles I, cast in 1633 by Le Sueur, had been prevented by the outbreak of civil war; it had been sold to a brazier who preserved it intact throughout the Commonwealth. In pursuance of his scheme to win over public opinion in favour of the new Parliament shortly to be convened, Danby himself bought it in 1675 and proposed to set it up in its present position at the top of Whitehall, close to his official residence at Wallingford House. The delay in carrying out the scheme, however, produced the satire that has generally been attributed to Marvell:

But why is the Work then so long at a stand?
Such Things you shou'd never, or suddenly do.
As the Parliament twice was Prorogu'd by your hand,
Will you venture so far to prorogue the King too?

The satire was first printed in *Poems upon Affairs of State*, Part 3, 1698, from which the lines quoted above are slightly adapted.

Controversialist in Prose

For this sharpness of Stile does indeed for the most part naturally flow from the humour of the Writer: and therefore tis observable that few are guilty of it but either those that write too young, (when it resembles the acidity of juices strain'd from the fruits before they be matured) or else those that write too old (and then 'tis like the sowrness of liquors which being near corrupting turn eager) And both these are generally disrellish'd: or if men do admit them for sawce, yet he must be very thirsty that will take a draught of 'm; whereas the generousest wine drops from the grape naturally without pressing, and though piquant hath its sweetness. And though I cannot arrogate so much as even the similitude of those good qualities to my Writing, yet I dare say that never was there a more pregnant ripeness in the causes.

The Rehearsall Transpros'd, Part II

THE only political pamphlet that Marvell is known to have published, *An Account of the Growth of Popery and Arbitrary Government* (1677), is wholly serious in manner, powerfully written and carefully documented. It opens with a description of the constitution of England, but the argument that is then developed implies plainly enough that Marvell, disillusioned with the Stuart monarchy, desired further curbs on the royal prerogative. The Popery that he detected in Court circles was in truth more a matter of pro-French intrigue than Vatican influence: Catholicism, especially in connection with the succession to the throne, concerned him nearly, but there were other enemies within the Anglican establishment.

There is no evidence that Marvell was ever a member of any Presbyterian or dissenting congregation, yet during the last six years of his life he took up his pen several times in their defence, or more accurately in defence of religious toleration in that quarter. His indignation was directed largely against the bishops and their refusal to slacken the requirements for conformity in matters of ceremony, but it could quickly be aroused with (as yet) lesser dignitaries, especially when they became abusive, like Parker, or rashly facetious, like Turner. The boisterous invective levelled against the former in two parts of *The Rehearsal Transpros'd* (1672–3) was moderated a little in *Mr. Smirke* (1676), in which Marvell defends a bishop who had advocated toleration, though a wholly serious case is made out in the appended *Essay on Councils*. Marvell's final pamphlet, entitled *Remarks upon a late disingenuous Discourse* (1678), moves into the realm of theology proper, where to be 'witty and entertaining' was unfortunately not enough.

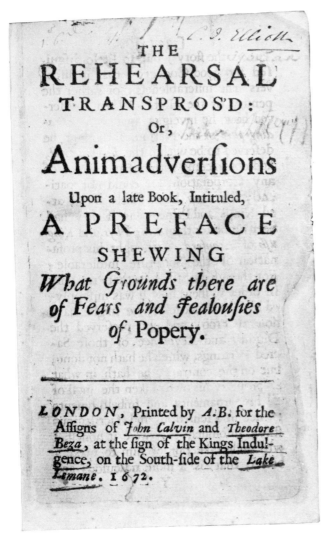

THE
REHEARSAL
TRANSPROS'D:
Or,
Animadverfions
Upon a late Book, Intituled,
A PREFACE
SHEWING
*What Grounds there are
of Fears and Jealoufies
of* Popery.

LONDON, Printed by *A.B.* for the
Affigns of *John Calvin* and *Theodore
Beza*, at the fign of the Kings Indul-
gence, on the South-fide of the *Lake
Lemane.* 1672.

Marvell's *The Rehearsal Transpros'd*, Part I, 1672 (96)

95 *Bishop Bramhall's Vindication of Himself and the Episcopal Clergy, from the Presbyterian Charge of Popery, as it is managed by Mr. Baxter in his Treatise of the Grotian Religion*, 1672

3938.aa.28.

Samuel Parker began his Oxford career as a fanatical Presbyterian but ended it as an Anglican whose anti-Puritan views became, in the following years, ever more bigoted. Marvell first

encountered him at Milton's house shortly after the Restoration. He soon rose in the Anglican Church thanks to his ready pen, which he employed against 'enthusiasm' and in support of the state religion and its enforcement by king and magistrates. His *Discourse of Ecclesiastical Polity* (1670) is a work in which, as the title proclaims, 'the authority of the Civil Magistrate over the consciences of subjects in matters of external religion is asserted, the mischiefs . . . of toleration are represented, and all pretenses pleaded in behalf of liberty of conscience are fully answered'. A reply by John Owen, the Independent minister, provoked a *Defence and Continuation* (1671) of the former work and in the following year Parker, by then Archdeacon and Prebend of Canterbury, continued his attack on dissenters with a lengthy preface written to accompany a hitherto unpublished tract by John Bramhall, Archbishop of Armagh (d. 1663). This finally brought Marvell into the controversy, with the first part of *The Rehearsal Transpros'd*.

96 *The Rehearsal Transpros'd*, Part I, 1672.
c.131.b.22.

The title of Marvell's witty, scurrilous and rambling 'animadversions' on Parker the man and the religious absolutist was, like the name of 'Bayes' with which he labelled his opponent, suggested by Buckingham's recent play, *The Rehearsal*. It was written during the autumn of 1672 and published soon after, anonymously and without licence: the first impression had sold out by the time that it was brought to the attention of Roger L'Estrange, the Surveyor of the Press. Part of a second impression was just then confiscated from the printer, Nathaniel Ponder, by the Stationers' Company; Ponder immediately called on the Lord Privy Seal, the Earl of Anglesey, who informed L'Estrange that it was the King's wish that the book should be 'allowed', 'for Parker has done him wrong, and this man has done him right' (see no. 97). L'Estrange was, however, unable to persuade the clerk of the Stationers' Company to enter the book in his register.

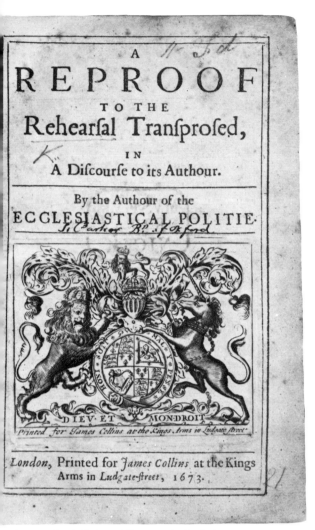

A
REPROOF
TO THE
Rehearsal Transprosed,
IN
A Discourse to its Authour.

By the Authour of the
ECCLESIASTICAL POLITIE.

DIEV ET MONDROIT
Printed for James Collins at the Kings Arms in Ludgate-street.

London, Printed for *James Collins* at the Kings Arms in *Ludgate-street*, 1673.

Parker's *Reproof to the Rehearsal Transprosed*, 1673 (99)

THE
REHEARSALL
TRANSPROS'D:
The SECOND PART.

Occasioned by Two Letters: The first Printed, by a nameless Author, Intituled, A Reproof, &c. The Second Letter left for me at a Friends House, Dated Nov. 3. 1673. *Subscribed* J. G. *and concluding with these words; If thou darest to Print or Publish any Lie or Libel against Doctor Parker, By the Eternal God I will cut thy Throat.*

Answered by ANDREW MARVEL

LONDON,
Printed for Nathaniel Ponder *at the* Peacock *in* Chancery Lane *near* Fleet-Street, 1673.

Marvell's *The Rehearsall Transpros'd*, Part II, 1673 (101)

Unfortunately for Parker the King had issued his Declaration of Indulgence in March 1672, which made his arguments something close to treasonable, as Marvell was able to point out. However, the Declaration was universally regarded with suspicion and dislike, even by the non-conformists whom it was aimed to win over, so that Charles was glad of the support afforded by Marvell's amusing burlesque. Burnet observed of Parker

His extravagant way of writing gave occasion to the wittiest books that have appeared in this age, for Mr. Marvell undertook him and treated him in ridicule in the severest but pleasantest manner possible, and by this one character one may judge how pleasant these books were; for the last King [Charles II], that was not a great reader of books, read them over and over again.

The present copy of *The Rehearsal Transpros'd* is the first impression of the edition, printed before L'Estrange authorised the suppressions that were not, in fact, made in the second impression, though the offending imprint 'for the Assigns of John Calvin and Theodore Beza' was removed.

BIBLIOGRAPHY: *The Rehearsal Transpros'd and the Rehearsall Transpros'd: the second part*, ed. by D. I. B. Smith (Oxford, 1972).

97 Henry Coventry's examination of Roger L'Estrange, 23 January 1673.

Finch MSS (Leicestershire Record Office): DG7 Box 4985.

L'Estrange declareth, that he neither knew, nor heard of *the Rehearsall Transprosd*, till the first Impression was distributed, and that Enquiring of one Brome, a Bookseller, about it, he told this Examinate, that it was printed for Ponder, who own'd the thing, and sayd that if the Book were Questioned, there were those would Justify it, and bring him off. Before this Examinate could meet with Ponder, there were two sheets of a second Impression seised at the Presse, by Mr Mearn, one of the Wardens of the Company of the Stationers; and thereupon Ponder came to L'Estrange, and told him of it and withall, that the Earle of Anglesey desired to speake with him; who took Ponder along with him Immediately to his Lordshipp at his house in Drury Lane: where the Earle was pleased to speake to the Examinate (in the presence, and (as he beleeves) in the hearing of Mr Ponder) in these or the like works. Look you M^r L'Estrange there is a Book come out, (*the Rehearsall Transpros'd*) I presume you have seen it.) I have spoken to his Majesty about it, and the King says *he will not have it suprest, for Parker has done him wrong, and this man has done him Right*: and I desired to speak with you to tell you this. And since the King will have the Book to passe, Pray give Mr Ponder your License to it, that it may not bee printed from him. To which, this Examinate Reply'd, that since it was his Majesty's pleasure, he would not meddle to give it any Interruption, but that there were some things in it not fit to be Licensed, Instancing in two Passages: viz: *the Roman Emperour's receiving a Dagger* Pag: 24 and *the wisdome of the King and Parliament Exposed* Pag: 310 whereupon his Lordshipp took the Book of Ponder, and upon perusall of those places agreed with this Examinate, that they were better out, then In, advising him withall, to Alter those places, letting the

body of the discourse remayne. To which, This Examinate made answere that he did not love to tamper with other mens Copyes, without the Privity and Allowance of the Author. His Lordshipp reply'd that he could not say any thing of the Author, but that such alterations might be made without him. And so this Examinate took Leave of the Earle and departed, with Ponder in his Company, who upon the way, desired L'Estrange to give him a note under his hand, of Signification to the Printers, what direction his Lordshipp had given him from his Majesty concerning this Book, which he did Accordingly.

The next work was to reade over the Book in Order to a License, which was done, (all but two or three sheets) in the presence of Ponder.

(From the papers of Sir Heneage Finch, Attorney General 1670–73, deposited by the late Lt. Col. J.R. Hanbury of Burley on the Hill.)

98 [Richard Leigh], *The Transproser Rehears'd*, 1673.

1077.d.39.

No fewer than six answers to the first part of Marvell's pamphlet appeared in print, the third in point of time being that commonly ascribed to a twenty-three year old graduate of Oxford, Richard Leigh, whose *Poems upon Several Occasions* (1675) seems to show in at least one place – the piece entitled 'Gathering Peaches' – an affinity with the elder poet. It is interesting to find, from a remark in the second part of his *Rehearsall Transpros'd*, that Marvell himself thought that this reply also was the work of Parker. What Leigh's interest was in the controversy, other than the aspiration of outburlesquing Marvell, we do not know, but he certainly outdid his rivals in downright indecency by hinting at an unnatural relationship between Marvell and Milton, in the following paraphrase (p. 135) of a French distich introduced into the controversy by Marvell himself:

O marvellous Fate, O Fate full of marvel;
That Nol's Latin Pay two Clerks should deserve ill!
Hiring a Gelding, and Milton the Stallion;
His Latin was gelt, and turn'd pure Italian.

99 Samuel Parker's *Reproof to the Rehearsal Transprosed*, 1673.

1019.i.22.

Parker's reply to the first part of *The Rehearsal Transpros'd* was entered in the Stationers' Register, by a curious irony, on 15 March 1673, a year to the day after the King had issued his Declaration of Indulgence. However, this had been withdrawn by a vote of the Commons a short time before the *Reproof* was envisaged, so that Parker was able to accuse Marvell in turn of rebellion against the will of Parliament. Otherwise he attempted to answer Marvell in his own manner, but scurrility got the better of wit, so that one feels some sympathy when his opponent complains that 'it is the rudest book . . . that ever was publisht . . .' (see no. 100). By early May it was out, and is listed in the Term Catalogues under the 6th of that month.

To students of Marvell's poetry the most interesting part of Parker's book is perhaps his asides on the man who had 'possessed wit and rithm these fifty years'. Refering to a specific charge of Marvell's, that after leaving Oxford he had ingratiated himself with the nobleman whom he served by continual invective against dissenters, Parker writes (p. 269):

And so we arrive at the Character of a Noble-man's Chaplain; for having heretofore (among other your juvenile Essays of Ballads, Poesies, Anagrams and Acrosticks) laid out your self upon this Subject also, and your Papers lying useless by you at this time when your Muse began to tire and set, it might be very convenient to fill up twelve pages with this Character whilst she baited and recover'd Breath.

100 Marvell's letter to Sir Edward Harley, 3 May 1673.

B.L. (Portland) Loan: 29/182, f.58.

. . . I find here at my returne a new booke against the Rehearsall intitled: S^t, to him Bayes: writ by one Hodges. But it is like the rest only somthing more triviall. Gregory Gray-beard is not yet out. Dr Parker will be out the next weeke. I have seen of it already 330 pages and it will be much more. I perceive by what I have read that it is the rudest book, one or other, that ever was publisht (I may

Marvell's letter to Sir Edward Harley, 3 May 1673 (100)

My Lords & Gentlemen

I could you last meeting the Winter was the fittest
time for busines, & I thought soe till my Lord Treasurer
assured me that the Spring is ye best Season for Sallets
& Subsidies, I hope therefore this Aprill will not
prove such an unnaturall moneth as not to afford some
kind Showres to refresh my parched Exchequer that
gapeth for want of them, but some of you may phaps
thinke it dangerous to make me too rich, but doe not
fear it I promise you faithfully what ever you giue
me I will always want, & though in other things
my word may be thought but slender security yet
in this you may rely upon me that I will not break
it.
  My Lords & Gentlemen I can bear my owne
straits wth patience but my Lord Treasurer doth
protest to me that the Revenue as it standeth will
not serue him & me to, one of us much pinch for it
If you doe not help us, I may speake truely to you
I am under incumbrances, for besides my whores in
service, my reformado whores lye hard upon me I
haue a pretty estate I confesse, but Gods fish I haue
a great charge upon it, here is my Lord Treasurer can
tell you that all the money designed for the Summer
Guard must of necessity be applyed to next yeares
Cradles & Swadling Clouts.
           onely
What shall we doe for Ships then? I hint to you for
that is your busines & not mine, I know by experience
that I can liue wthout ships, I liued 10 yeares abroad
wthout Ships & had never better health in my life
but how well you will doe wth out them I leaue to ye
selues to Judge, therefore I doe not insist upon it.
Othere is another thing I must presse more earnestly
wch is this, it seemes a good part of my Revenue will
faile me in 3 yeares except you will please to continue it
now I haue this to say, pray why did you giue soe much
as you haue done except you resolved beforehand to giue me
as fast as I shall ask you, the nation hates you for
having giuen soe much already & she hate you now

say), since the first invention of printing. Although it handles me so roughly yet I am not at all amated by it. But I must desire the advice of some few friends to tell me whether it will be proper for me and in what way to answer it. However I will for mine own private satisfaction forthwith draw up an answer that shall have as much of spirit and solidity in it as my ability will afford & the age we live in will indure. I am (if I may say it with reverence) drawn in, I hope by a good Providence, to intermeddle in a noble and high argument which therefore by how much it is above my capacity I shall use the more industry not to disparage it. But I desire that all the discourse of my friends may run as if no answer ought to be expected to so scurrilous a book . . .

101 *The Rehearsall Transpros'd*, Part II, 1673.
G.19515.

This reply to Parker's *Reproof* appeared under Marvell's name but was entered neither in the Stationers' Register nor the Term Catalogues, being no doubt tacitly allowed. It was published in two editions, of which that shown here was the first, and it effectively silenced Parker. Summing up the controversy in his account of the future Bishop of Oxford Anthony Wood observed that

. . . it was generally thought, nay even by many of those who were otherwise favourers of Parker's cause, that he (Parker) thro' a too loose and unwary handling of the debate (tho' in a brave, flourishing and lofty stile) laid himself too open to the severe strokes of his sneering adversary, and that the odds and victory lay on Marvell's side: Howsoever it was, it wrought this good effect upon our author, that for ever after it took down somewhat of his high spirit, insomuch that tho' Marvell in a second part replied upon our author's reproof, yet he judged it more prudent rather to lay down the cudgels, than to enter the lists again with an untowardly combatant so hugely well vers'd and experienc'd in the then, but newly, refin'd art (tho' much in mode and fashion almost ever since) of sportive and jeering buffoonry. . . .

102 Samuel Parker, *History of his own Time*, 1727.
292.i.26.

Parker's Latin work, left in manuscript at his death, was published in 1726 and in a translation by Thomas Newlin in the following year. This account of Marvell, which can claim to be the second surviving biographical notice in point of composition, is a mixture of scurrility with some fact, partly misrepresented and perhaps partly misunderstood. The kernel of it runs as follows.

Amongst these lewd Revilers, the lewdest was one whose name was *Marvel*. As he had liv'd in all manner of wickedness from his youth, so being of a singular impudence and petulancy of nature, he exercised the province of a Satyrist . . . Being abandon'd by his father, and expell'd the University, . . . A vagabond, ragged, hungry Poetaster, ... At length, by the interest of *Milton*, to whom he was somewhat agreeable for his ill-natur'd wit, he was made Undersecretary to *Cromwell's* Secretary. . . . But the King being restor'd, this wretched man falling into his former poverty, did, for the sake of a livelihood, procure himself to be chosen Member of Parliament for a Borough, in which his father had exercis'd the office of a Presbyterian teacher . . . . In all Parliaments he was an enemy to the King's affairs . . . . But out of the House, when he could do it with impunity, he vented himself with the greater bitterness, and daily spewed infamous libels out of his filthy mouth against the King himself . . . . But this *Bustuarius*, or fencer, never fought with more fury, than near his own grave, in a book written a little before his death, to which he gave this title, [An Account of the Growth of Popery, and Arbitrary Government in England].

103 'His Majesty's Most Gracious Speech to both Houses of Parliament', 13 April 1675.
Stowe MS 180, f.77.

Writing to the Corporation of Hull on the first day of the thirteenth session of the Cavalier Parliament, Marvell outlined the King's speech, concluding with these words: 'And I must desire you not by this summary relation I give you . . . to conceive of it accordingly. For by reason of the shortnesse of my memory and conception I do it much wrong both as to the matter and the expression. When printed I will send it you'. The irony was no doubt lost on his constituents who must have been unaware that he had some time before the session opened written a mock speech in anticipation of the content of Charles's, and the accuracy of his forecast probably afforded him much gratification.

that they were being produced in some numbers for circulation. The speech was first attributed to Marvell in *Poems on Affairs of State*, 1704, Part III, pp. 84 et seq., whence it was printed by Cooke and, following him, Thompson. Other contemporary manuscript versions are found in PRO *SP Dom. Car. II*, 369, *No.* 197, and Harley MSS 1579, ff.136,1366 and 7315, ff.98b–102. The transcript found in Add. MS 34362 is followed by a similar essay of 1681 which shows the same traits, though not so entertainingly.

104 *An Account of the Growth of Popery, and Arbitrary Government in England.* 1677.
Ashley 1104.

Marvell's tract, which was ostensibly printed at Amsterdam and published soon after Christmas 1677, is in effect a political history of England for the period noted in the subtitle, together with the parliamentary session that ended on 8 December. It is of course biased, being written on the thesis that 'There has now for divers years a design been carried on to change the lawful Government of England into an absolute Tyranny, and to convert the established Protestant Religion into downright Popery'. With the exception of two now unknown to history the names of the conspirators are nowhere mentioned, but the King is diplomatically absolved of blame as regards the attempt to establish a tyranny by references to 'that felicity, which hath always attended him, when excluding the corrupt politicks of others he hath followed the dictates of his own royal wisdom . . .' The heroes of the story are the four lords who were committed to the Tower for questioning the legality of the prorogation (see no. 79), and more especially the Earl of Shaftesbury who, though still imprisoned at the time of writing, was not 'as yet' – the adverb points a moral – 'a Martyr for the *English* Liberties and the Protestant Religion'.

105 Marvell's letter to William Popple, 10 June 1678.
C.95.a.16.

Cooke's edition of 1726 (vol. II, pp. 70–1) is the sole authority for Marvell's last-known personal

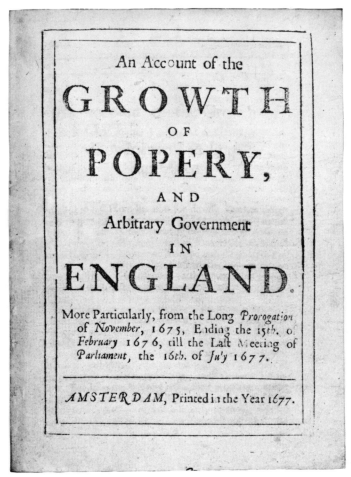

Marvell's *Account of the Growth of Popery*, 1677 (104)

The political aim of the performance seems to have been nothing less than to provoke a quarrel between the King and Commons; its comedy depends largely upon Marvell's putting into the King's mouth an ingenuous avowal of the more personal and scandalous reasons of his latest appeal for funds. There is every chance, moreover, that he took pains to capture Charles's peculiarities of address: may we see in this essay of Marvell's a dramatist *manqué*?

The present manuscript is copied on the same stock of paper as one in Egerton MS 3345, ff. 21, 22, and this, plus the fact they are written in different but evidently scribal hands, suggests letter, in which, as in a previous letter to Harley concerning Mr. Smirke, he writes of himself in the third person.

There came out, about Christmass last, here a large Book concerning *the Growth of Popery and Arbitrary Government*. There have been great Rewards offered in private, and considerable in the Gazette, to any who could inform of the Author or Printer, but not yet discovered. Three or four printed Books since have described, as near as it was proper to go, the Man being a Member of Parliament, Mr. *Marvell* to have been the Author; but if he had, surely he should not have escaped being questioned in Parliament, or some other Place.

The *London Gazette*, no. 1288, for 21–5 March 1678, carried an advertisement offering a reward of £50 for anyone informing on the printer or publisher, but £100 for identifying the 'Hander of it to the Press'.

106 Letter of Roger L'Estrange to Sir Joseph Williamson, 23 August 1678.

Public Record Office: SP29/406, f.49.

S^r/ with much difficulty I have found out the Widow Brewsters Lodging, I can prove against her, the bringing of Three Libells to the Presse in Manuscript: viz. *The Letter about the Test; The Two Speeches of the D: of Buck: and the Ld Shaftesbury, and Jenks his Speech*; upon which Accompt, she hath so long conceald her selfe. She is in the House of a person formerly an officer under Cromwell: one that writes three or foure very good Hands, and owns to have been employd in Transcribing things for a Counsellor in the Temple. From which Circumstances one may fayrly presume that all those Delicate Copyes, which Brewster carryed to the Presse, were written by Brewsters Land Lord, and Copyd by him, from the Authour. Beside that it is very probable, that the late Libells concerning the Growth of Popery, and the List of the Members of Parliament past through the same hands. This is humbly to begg your Honours Command what to do in this Case. If she be questiond, probably shee will cast the whole, upon Mr Marvell, who is lately dead; and there the enquiry ends. I was twice to attend you S^r, with this Enformation, but you were the 1st time abroad, and the 2d in Kent. This, with my humble Duty to you, is All from S^r, your Honours most Obedient Servant

Roger L'Estrange.

Italian, that brought him certain Letters, to the *B. stille*; he still remains there, and the Prince, as we are told, is resolved to discover the bottom of that matter.

WHereas there have been lately Printed, and Published several Seditious, and Scandalous Libels against the Proceedings of Both Houses of Parliament, and other His Majesties Courts of Justice, to the Dishonour of His Majesties Government, and the Hazard of the Publick Peace: These are to give Notice, That what Person soever shall Discover unto one of the Secretaries of State, the Printer, Publisher, Author, or Hander to the Press of any of the said Libels, so that full Evidence may be made thereof to a Jury, without mentioning the Informer; especially one Libel, Intituled, An Account of the Growth of Popery, &c. And another call'd, A Seasonable Argument to all the Grand Juries, &c. the Discoverer shall be rewarded as follows: He shall have Fifty Pounds for such Discovery, as aforesaid, of the Printer, or the Publisher of it from the Press; and for the Hander of it to the Press One hundred Pounds. And if it fall out that the Discoverer be a Master, or a Journyman-Printer, he shall be Authorized (in case of tracing the Proof up to the Author) to Set up a Printing-House for himself; and no Agent either in the Printing, Publishing, or Dispersing of the said Libels, shall be Punished for so doing, in case he shall contribute toward the Discovery of the Author of any such Libel.

Advertisements.

☞ **All for Love: Or, the World well Lost.**
A Tragedy, as it is Acted at the Theatre Royal And written in imitation of *Shakespear's* Stile. By *John Dryden,* Servant to His Majesty. Sold by *H. Herringman,* at the *Blue Anchor* in the *Lower Walk* of the *New Exchange.*

THese are to give Notice, That the General Post-Office is removed from *Bishopsgate-street,* to *Lombard-street,* to Sir Robert Viner's *House.*

London Gazette, 21–5 March 1678 (105)

Arms: Or, a chevron engrailed between three leopards' faces sable.
Crest: Out of a ducal coronet or, a plume of feathers argent.

Death and Aftermath

A Man so endowd by Nature, So improv'd by Education, Study & Travel, So consummated by Practice & Experience; That joining the most peculiar Graces of Wit and Learning, With a singular Penetration and strength of Judgement; And exercising all these, in the whole Course of his Life, With an unalterable Steadiness in the ways of Virtue; He became the Ornament & Example of his Age; Belov'd by Good Men, fear'd by Bad, admir'd by All; thô imitated, alas, by few, and scarse fully parallel'd by any.

Epitaph composed by William Popple

IN or about June 1677 Marvell, who then had lodgings in Maiden Lane, Covent Garden, persuaded his former landlady Mary Palmer to lease a house in Great Russell Street for the purpose of concealing from their creditors two city friends, partners in a firm of merchants who had recently been declared bankrupt. Although he also incurred the risk of helping to conceal part of their personal assets, all might have passed off smoothly but for his sudden death on 16 August 1678 at the house in Bloomsbury: he was buried two days later in St Giles-in-the-Fields.

Mary Palmer, acting in concert with the bankrupts, who wished to recover their money, convinced a court that she had been since May 1667 Marvell's wife by a clandestine marriage, and successfully obtained the administration of his estate. Unfortunately the church register that might have substantiated her claim is now missing, and since her confederates, who subsequently quarrelled with her, describe her as a person 'of mean condition' and no education, biographers have preferred not to believe in the marriage. Nevertheless it is to Mary Palmer that posterity owes the slim folio volume entitled 'Miscellaneous Poems. By *Andrew Marvell*, Esq; Late Member of the Honourable House of Commons. *London*, Printed for *Robert Boulter*, at the *Turks-Head* in *Cornhill*. M.DC.LXXXI.'

This posthumously published collection of verse is the prime, and for the vast majority of lyrical poems the only, witness to what Marvell actually wrote. It was published by Mary Palmer alias Marvell, as her note dated 15 October 1680 states, 'according to the exact Copies of my late dear Husband, under his own Hand-Writing, being found since his Death among his other Papers . . .' The book was advertised for sale in January 1681 and a copy that belonged to Narcissus Luttrell bears the date 18 January. British Library C.59.i.8 (see no. 29) is the most complete exemplar known, since it includes texts of two and a half of the three Cromwell poems that circumspection or the censor excluded from all other copies; while that which is now Huntingdon Library 79660 contains all but the half-poem (*A Poem upon the Death of O.C.*, ll. 1–184).

In the thirty years after his death, Marvell was not forgotten either by his friends or his enemies. Though the monument voted by Hull Corporation may never have been erected, or if so was torn down shortly thereafter, his prose pamphlets and the verse-satires attributed to him were frequently reprinted into the following century. His poems and letters were published, with a brief biographical notice, by Thomas 'Hesiod' Cooke in 1726, and precisely fifty years later, his name having been kept alive by Whig propagandists, Captain Edward Thompson RN did him the kindness of editing his poems, prose-works and letters in three handsome volumes.

107 John Morris' lease of two houses in Great Russell Street, 20 September 1676.
Loaned by the Trustees of the Bedford Estates.

John Morris, described as 'nailor' of the Parish of St Giles-in-the-Fields, leased from Lady Rachel Vaughan for the term of forty-two years two houses on the north side of Great Russell Street in September 1676. Lady Vaughan was one of the three daughters and co-heirs of the last Earl of Southampton (d.1667), and her property passed by marriage to the Russell family in the following century. One of these two houses was sub-let 'about the month of June' 1677 to Andrew Marvell, in the name of his housekeeper Mary Palmer, but the sub-lease has not been traced and the house cannot be identified.

The household at Great Russell Street thus consisted of Marvell, the bankrupts Nelthorpe and Thompson, the latter's wife Dorothy, Mary Palmer and a servant under her. It was here that Marvell died in August 1678. During the Chancery suits that followed his death, Mary Palmer asserted 'That for severall yeares before [1677] she this Defendent dwelt in and kept a house in Westminster where the said Andrew Marvell dwelt with her (in truth as her husband) though he might be generally lookt upon only as a Lodger at her house'. She claimed that her clandestine marriage with Marvell had taken place 'on or about' 13 May 1667 at the church of the Holy Trinity in the Little Minories, and though the Court accepted this her claim cannot now be verified, owing to the loss of the relevant register.

Both houses in Great Russell Street would be of three stories, probably with a basement, and had frontages of twenty feet, stretching back one hundred and fifty feet to the bottom of their walled gardens, which were canted from the line of the street. They were doubtless very similar in appearance to those immediately adjoining Southampton House, shown in Sutton Nicholls' view in Bowles' *Prospects of the Most Considerable Buildings about London*, 1725. One of them, described in a later lease as the fifth house westward from Montagu house, was already part of a terrace that consisted of six or eight houses, whilst the other, subsequently the tenth in a row that came to comprise eleven, was in September 1676 flanked by two dwellings that were still under construction. The former house stood slightly to the west of, but bordering on, the site of the present Director's Residence of the British Museum: the other is now part of no. 92, itself occupying the site of the tenth and part of the eleventh house, the latter having been demolished to make way for Charlotte Street, now Bloomsbury Street. Numbers 89 to 91, on the site of the seventh to ninth houses in Marvell's day, remain substantially as they were in the rebuilding of about 1780.

108 The parish of St Giles-in-the-Fields, about 1676–80.
Map Library: Crace Port. II. 58.

William Morgan succeeded his kinsman John Ogilby as Cosmographer Royal, and produced his 'London, Actually Survey'd . . . 1681/2' as the successor to the other's map of 1676. The scale is three hundred feet to the inch, and upon the ground plan of the streets are superimposed elevations of some prominent buildings. Thus, St Giles's church is seen from the south, accurately enough represented in outline but possibly somewhat deficient in the number and

The church of St Giles-in-the-Fields from the north, 1719 (110)

disposition of the windows in the south aisle, which do not correspond with those of a later view from the north (see no. 56), or with that of Hollar (see no. 78).

By the later 1670s Great Russell Street, then the northernmost limit of London's encroachment at that point, was only sparsely built up on the north side, from which open fields stretched to Camden and Hampstead. The house that Marvell 'pitched upon' in 1677 thus afforded pleasant views and amenities. Most of the eastern end of the street was taken up with Southampton House, which stood at the top of Bloomsbury Square, and Montagu House, later to become the British Museum. Morgan's map shows seven houses standing westward from Montagu house, each having a long walled garden at the rear: though this was probably the case when his map was surveyed, by 1681/2 the number had been increased to eleven, as is shown by the terms of Morris's lease (see no.

107). Moreover, the width of the houses is rather exaggerated in Morgan's representation.

BIBLIOGRAPHY: I. Darlington and J. Howgego, *Printed Maps of London*, (London, 1964).

109 Dr Richard Morton's account of Marvell's death, 1692.

776.c.7.

In July 1678 Marvell visited Hull, leaving for London on 9 August. While on the road he was seized by an attack of tertian ague and on his arrival in Great Russell Street summoned a doctor, who bled him. What follows is recounted in Latin in Richard Morton's Πυρετολογια, a general treatise on fevers, published in 1692:

The way having been made ready after this fashion, at the beginning of the next fit [the fourth, that is, of tertian ague] a great febrifuge was administered, that is to say, a draught of Venice treacle, etc. By the doctor's orders the patient was covered up close with blankets, or rather buried under them; and composed himself to sleep and sweat, in order to escape the cold shivers that ordinarily accompany the onset of the ague-fit. Seized with the profoundest sleep and sweating profusely, in the short space of twenty-four hours after the last fit he died comatose [*Apopleptice*]. Thus the patient died who, had a single ounce of Peruvian bark been properly administered, might easily have escaped, in twenty four hours, from the jaws of death and the grave. This is what I, burning with anger, informed the doctor when he told me this story without any sense of shame.

Unfortunately for Marvell his doctor, whom Morton describes as a conceited old man, held Peruvian bark in contempt. Morton's indignation was not merely professional: he admired Marvell and calls his death a great loss to the world of letters. As a former minister, ejected for refusal to subscribe to the Act of Uniformity, and a fellow of the Royal College of Physicians whose name was omitted from James II's Charter, his religious and political views are likely to have chimed with those of the other.

110 The Church of St Giles-in-the-Fields, 1719.

B.M. Department of Prints and Drawings: Pennant VII, p. 9.

Marvell died in the house that he had taken in Great Russell Street on 16 August 1678 and two days later was buried in St Giles' church. Anthony Wood learned from the sexton that he 'lies interred under the Pewes in the south side . . . under the window wherein is painted in glasse a red lyon, [it was given by the Inneholder of the red Lyon Inne in Holborne] and is the [blank] window from the east' (see no. 82). From the 1720 edition of Stowe's *Survey of London* (II, 78) we gather that the third window from the top of the south isle was 'Glazed at the Charge of Mr. *John Johnson*, Inn-keeper, in *High Holborn*, 1625' and bears the figure of a lion in the wilderness.

This drawing of the old church from the north was taken from an original, that was signed 'John Hall Med Temple Lond Marti 17 1718', by John Thomas Smith (1766–1833),

Entry of Marvell's burial in the register of St Giles's, 18 August 1678 (110)

Keeper of Prints and Drawings at the British Museum. A lithograph from the same drawing was executed by George Scharf (Department of Prints and Drawings: Crace Port. XXVIII, 116). A view from the south is shown in Morgan's map (see no. 108). The old church, which replaced an earlier one, had been built between 1623 and 1631, when it was consecrated by Archbishop Laud; it was itself replaced by the present church, built in 1731–3 by Henry Flitcroft in exactly the same position.

BIBLIOGRAPHY: L.C.C. Survey of London, *Parish of St. Giles-in-the-Fields (Pt.2)*, 1914, pp.127–140; Stowe's *Survey of the Cities of London and Westminster*, rev. by John Strype, vol. 2, pp. 75–85, (London, 1720).

111 Anonymous verses 'On his Excellent Friend Mr. Andrew Marvell', 1678

1473.c.42.

This poem, which was first printed in *Poems on Affairs of State*, 1697, is the first work published after Marvell's death that singles him out for commendation expressly on the grounds of his patriotism, the virtue for which he was remembered throughout the century that followed. In it Marvell, 'this island's watchful sentinel', is saluted as the man who 'th' approach of Rome did first deplore And the grim monster, arbitrary pow'r', doubtless with reference to the *Account of the Growth of Popery and Arbitrary Power* that was published in the year of his death. The anonymous author goes even further and does not hesitate to compare him with Socrates and Cicero, on account of his moral rectitude and fearless eloquence, concluding with some rather Miltonic lines that spring from current suspicions about the cause of his death:

But whether Fate or Art untwin'd his thread,
Remains in doubt. Fames lasting Register
Shall leave his Name enroll'd as great as theirs,
Who in *Philippi* for their Country fell.

The text shown (and quoted) here is that of *Poems on Affairs of State*, 1699.

BIBLIOGRAPHY: *Poems on Affairs of State*, ed. by George de F. Lord, vol. 1 (1660–78), pp. 436–7 (Yale, 1963).

112 John Ayloffe, 'Marvell's Ghost', about 1678.
Add. MS 23722, ff.22b,23.

The assumed author of this indictment of the Stuarts matriculated either at St. Edmund Hall, Oxford, in 1662, or at Trinity College, Cambridge, in 1666, subsequently enrolling at the Inner Temple. He was a daring patriot who during the debates on foreign policy in 1673 had placed by the Speaker's chair a wooden shoe, the symbol of slavery. Together with Marvell he belonged to a Dutch fifth-column organised by William of Orange's secretary, Peter du Moulin, to alert the House of Commons to the dangers of Charles's pro-French and pro-Catholic policy (see no. 71). After being involved in the Rye House Plot he fled to Scotland, where he was captured two years later, and on 30 October 1685 was executed at the gate of the Inner Temple.

Ayloffe's political satires in verse survive in contemporary manuscript collections. In the present verses the ghost of his patriotic friend is made to return to earth 'To acquaynt poor England with her doom'.

A brace of Exil'd youths (whose fates
Shall pull down vengeance on those states
That Harbour'd them abroad) must come
Well skilld in forreign vices home.
And shall their dark designs to hide,
With two contesting Churches side.
Till, with cross persecuting Zeal,
They have destroy'd the Common Weal.

The manuscript of political satires in which these lines, along with others commonly ascribed to Marvell, occur was transcribed about 1679–80.

BIBLIOGRAPHY: K.H.D. Haley, *William of Orange and the English Opposition 1672–4*, (Oxford, 1953).

113 'The severall Answeare of Mary Marvell widdow one of the defendants to the Bill of complaint of John Farrington, Complainant'.
Public Record Office: C6/276/48 (2).

Marvell seems to have forwarded a bill in the Commons that made his bankrupt friends secure from prosecution until Easter 1678, and, with far less justification, connived at concealing some part of their personal assets by allowing Nelthorpe to make out a goldsmith's bond for five hundred pounds in his name.

His unexpected decease in August 1678 was followed a month later by that of Nelthorpe. A year later his housekeeper, Mary Palmer, acting in agreement with the remaining bankrupts and successfully claiming in court to be Marvell's widow, obtained the administration of his estate. In the summer of 1681, however, she quarrelled with one of the number, John Farrington. The present suit is one of several that were subsequently filed in Chancery on both sides: Mary Palmer's account of Marvell's financial assets may be rather exaggerated.

. . . this defendant sayth that the said Mr Nelthorpe after he had withdrawn himselfe from his habitation in London he did for som time cohabitt and live with the said Andrew Marvell att his house in Great Russell Street . . . and that he the said Andrew Marvell also had a lodging for his privacy in Mayden Lane in

TO THE
R E A D E R.

Thefe are to Certifie every Ingenious Reader, that all thefe Poems, as alfo the other things in
this Book contained, are Printed according
to the exact Copies of my late dear Husband, under his own Hand-Writing, being
found fince his Death among his other Papers, Witnefs my Hand this 15*th* day of
October, 1680.

Mary Marvell.

Mary Palmer's note in *Miscellaneous Poems*, 1681 (113)

Engraved portrait of Marvell from *Miscellaneous Poems*, 1681 (114)

MISCELLANEOUS
POEMS.

BY
ANDREW MARVELL, Efq;
Late Member of the Honourable Houſe of Commons.

LONDON,
Printed for *Robert Boulter*, at the *Turks-Head*
in *Cornhill*. M. DC. LXXXI.

Title-page of *Miscellaneous Poems*, 1681 (114)

Covent Garden where he kept his money bonds bills Jewells writeings & other goods & chattles and that the said Andrew Marvell about the sixteenth of August [1678] dyed intestate at the house where he lived in Russell Street possessed of a considerable personall Estate consisting in money Jewells bonds bills & otherwise to a good value (as this defendant hath reason to believe) and in particular at the time of his death left in his study & att his Lodgings in Mayden Lane many trunks & Hampers wherein were great Summes of money in Gold & Silver besides bonds bills books Jewells and other goods of value . . . and this defendant going afterwards to look for her husbands Estate and shee finding no Estate of her husbands but a few Bookes & papers of a small value was dissatiffyed therein . . .

BIBLIOGRAPHY: Fred S. Tupper, 'Mary Palmer, alias Mrs. Andrew Marvell', *Publications of the Modern Language Association of America*, LIII (1938), pp. 367–92.

114 Engraved portrait of Marvell from *Miscellaneous Poems*, 1681.
Ashley 4898.

The engraving of Marvell that was published as the frontispiece to the *Miscellaneous Poems* must be considered as the touchstone for all other representations whatever, since it was executed for his housekeeper (or wife) less than three years after his death. If it were spurious, the fact would probably have been noted by one of the many people still living at that time who had known him.

Though in some ways akin to the Hollis portrait, the engraving is probably based on the Nettleton one: the anonymous engraver has reversed the image by cutting his block directly after the portrait, and has altered the original in various other ways. These include giving the subject a cloak over his jacket, bringing into prominence a row of buttons not easily visible there, discarding the skull cap and giving the hair the appearance of a peruke. Perhaps this last touch, together with the slight ageing that can be detected in the features, represents an attempt to bring the early Restoration image closer to his actual appearance at death.

The identity of the engraver is unknown, but the presentation is entirely of the period. We may compare Faithorne's engraving of Cowley in the *Works* of 1668, re-engraved by the same craftsman in 1687.

BIBLIOGRAPHY: D. Piper, *op. cit.*, pp. 221–2.

115 Popple's epitaph for Marvell, 1688.
Add. MS 8888, f.86.

William Popple (d. 1708), Marvell's favourite nephew, and grandfather of the dramatist of the same name (see no. 52), included this epitaph for 'my uncle Marvell' in a volume of scribal transcripts of his verse-translations and original poems that are there dated to between 1681 and 1701. The text was printed thus in Cooke's edition of 1726, but another version, which has some differences of wording towards the end and lacks the concluding Latin distich, was set up in St Giles's church in 1764 by Marvell's grand-nephew Robert Nettleton, being included also in Thompson's edition of 1776.

In the present manuscript, which was copied by two scribes, the epitaph is dated 1688 and is thus difficult to identify with that written, or intended to be written, for the monument voted by Hull Corporation on 24 September 1678, though Popple explicitly mentions such a commission. The assumption of error in the dating seems, moreover, to be ruled out by the chronological arrangement of the pieces, that begins with 1681. Yet there remains some doubt that a monument was ever erected in the year of Marvell's death, one tradition saying that the vicar would not countenance it: another, however, implies that it was, asserting that it was torn down by 'zealots of the King's party'.

NEAR UNTO THIS PLACE ⬭ LYETH THE BODY OF
ANDREW MARVELL ESQUIRE, A MAN SO ENDOWED BY NATURE
SO IMPROVED BY EDUCATION, STUDY & TRAVELL, SO CONSUMMATED
BY PRACTICE & EXPERIENCE; THAT JOINING THE MOST PECULIAR GRACES
OF WIT & LEARNING WITH A SINGULAR PENETRATION, & STRENGTH OF
JUDGMENT, & EXERCISING ALL THESE IN THE WHOLE COURSE OF HIS LIFE,
WITH AN UNALTERABLE STEADINESS IN THE WAYS OF VIRTUE, HE BECAME
THE ORNAMENT & EXAMPLE OF HIS AGE; BELOVED BY GOOD MEN, FEAR'D
BY BAD, ADMIR'D BY ALL, THO IMITATED ALASS! BY FEW, & SCARCE FULLY
PARALLELLED BY ANY, BUT A TOMB STONE CAN NEITHER CONTAIN HIS CHARACTER,
NOR IS MARBLE NECESSARY TO TRANSMIT IT TO POSTERITY, IT WILL BE ALWAYS
LEGIBLE IN HIS INIMITABLE WRITINGS, HE SERVED THE TOWN OF KINGSTON
UPON HULL, ABOVE 20 YEARS SUCCESSIVELY IN PARLIAMENT, & THAT, WITH SUCH
WISDOM, DEXTERITY, INTEGRITY & COURAGE AS BECOMES A TRUE PATRIOT,
HE DYED THE 16. AUGUST 1678 IN THE 58TH YEAR OF HIS AGE.
SACRED
TO THE MEMORY OF ANDREW MARVELL ESQ^R AS A STRENUOUS ASSERTER OF
THE CONSTITUTION, LAWS & LIBERTIES OF ENGLAND,
AND OUT OF FAMILY AFFECTION & ADMIRATION OF
THE UNCORRUPT PROBITY OF HIS LIFE & MANNERS
ROBERT NETTLETON OF LONDON MERCHANT, HIS GRAND NEPHEW
HATH CAUSED THIS SMALL MEMORIAL OF HIM,
TO BE ERECTED IN THE YEAR 1764.

Monument to Marvell
in St Giles's church, 1764 (115)

Select Bibliography

Major editions of Marvell's poetry and prose

Miscellaneous Poems, 1681.

The first collected edition, published after Marvell's death by his 'widow' Mary Palmer. Prints, mostly for the first time, fifty-one lyric and occasional poems in English or Latin, together with four prose epitaphs of which three are in Latin, one of them being accompanied by a covering letter in English. Three poems on Cromwell were cancelled from most copies before publication.

In 1969 the Scolar Press published a photographic facsimile of the completest copy (BL C.59.i.8), followed by manuscript texts of the three Cromwell poems from Bodleian MS Eng. poet. d. 49, a revised and enlarged copy of the 1681 Folio, together with those pages from the printed part that include annotations.

Works, ed. by Thomas Cooke, 2 vols., 1726; reprinted 1772.

Includes the poems and epitaphs of the 1681 Folio, together with two juvenile pieces in Latin and Greek, a selection of satires taken from *State Poems*, the mock speech of the King and a few private letters. The whole is prefaced by a life of Marvell.

Works, ed. by Capt. Edward Thompson, 3 vols., 1776.

Includes all the poems and letters in Cooke's edition, together with texts of the three Cromwell poems taken from what is now the Bodleian MS, and some new poems and satires, mostly spurious. A few new private letters, with the bulk of those to Hull Corporation, were printed, along with all the generally-accepted prose pamphlets plus three others, of which one is in Latin. There is also a life which was based partly on material collected by Thomas Hollis for a projected edition of Marvell's works.

Complete Works in Verse and Prose, ed. by A. B. Grosart, 4 vols., 1872–5 *(Fuller's Worthies Library)*.

The most complete single collection. Besides reprinting all the authentic prose works and most of the poems in Thompson's edition Grosart added the Trinity House letters, with a few others. His 'Memorial Introduction' included new biographical facts and several illustrations.

Poems and Letters, ed. by H. M. Margoliouth, 2 vols., Oxford 1927; 2nd edn., 1952; 3rd edn., rev. by Pierre Legouis and E. E. Duncan-Jones, 1971 *(Oxford English Texts)*.

Includes all the lyric or occasional poems by or attributed to Marvell, plus the epitaphs from the 1681 Folio and seventeen post-Restoration satires, of which, however, Margoliouth rejects two. This has since its first appearance been regarded as the standard edition of the poems and letters largely because of its comprehensiveness, textual collations and extensive commentary. The latter was enlarged in the third edition, which takes account of work published up to 1970, but the text was left substantially as in the 1952 revision. The collation of the satires has been partly superseded by Lord's edition of *Poems on Affairs of State*, and that of the lyrics to some extent by Donno (see below).

Complete Poetry, ed. by George de F. Lord, New York, 1968.

> Follows the Bodleian MS sparingly in its revised readings but more extensively in its attributions, especially of the post-Reformation satires, in which Lord largely ratifies his decision in *Poems on Affairs of State*, vol. 1 (1660–78), New Haven, 1963, though adding 'The King's Vows'. He rejects *Scaevola Scoto-Britannus*, which he does not print, and includes as of 'Doubtful Authorship' the Villiers elegy, 'Thyrsis *and* Dorinda', '*Tom May's* Death' and '*On the Victory obtained by* Blake *over the* Spaniards'.

Complete Poems, ed. by Elizabeth Story Donno, 1972 (*Penguin English Poets*).

> Prints as Marvell's all the lyrics and ocassional poems included in Margoliouth's edition, rejecting all satires but 'The Last Instructions' and 'The Loyall Scot' (in its fullest version), and including as of 'Uncertain Attribution' the Blood epigrams. Adopts more readings from the Bodleian MS than any other edition, and includes collations, though partial, of manuscripts of the lyrics not elsewhere recorded.

The Latin Poetry, translated by William A. McQueen and Kiffin A. Rockwell, Chapel Hill, North Carolina, 1964.

> An annotated edition of the Latin poems, in the text established by Margoliouth (1952), with line-for-line renderings into English that are of variable accuracy.

Concordance to the poetry

A Concordance to the English Poems of Andrew Marvell, compiled by G. R. Guffey, Chapel Hill, North Carolina, 1974. Based on Margoliouth (1952).

Bibliographies of the early editions

In Pierre Legouis, *André Marvell*, 1928 (see below), pp.451–471.

In A. F. Allison, *Four Metaphysical Poets*, 1973 (*Pall Mall Bibliographies*).

> Described as 'A Bibliographical Catalogue of the Early Editions of [the] Poetry and Prose (To the end of the 17th century).

Bibliographical and critical studies (full-length only)

Pierre Legouis, *André Marvell: poète, puritain, patriote*, Paris and London, 1928. Abridged and brought up to date as *Andrew Marvell*, Oxford, 1st edn. 1965; 2nd edn. 1968.

> The standard biographical study, including an interpretation of the literary works and a bibliography of editions, books and articles relating to Marvell.

M. C. Bradbrook and M. G. Lloyd-Thomas, *Andrew Marvell*, Cambridge, 1940; reprinted with corrections 1961.

H. E. Toliver, *Marvell's Ironic Vision*, New Haven, Connecticut, 1965.

J. B. Leishman, *The Art of Marvell's Poetry*, 1966; 2nd. edn. 1968.

J. M. Wallace, *Destiny his choice: the loyalism of Andrew Marvell*, Cambridge, 1968.

Ann E. Berthoff, *The Resolved Soul*, Princeton,1970.

Rosemary Colie, '*My Echoing Song*', Princeton, 1970.

Donald M. Friedman, *Marvell's Pastoral Art*, 1970.

Bruce King, *Marvell's allegorical poetry*, 1977.

Kenneth Friedenreich (ed.), *Tercentenary Essays in Honor of Andrew Marvell*, Hamden, Conn., 1977.

John Dixon Hunt, *Andrew Marvell: his life and writings*, 1978.

Selections of critical essays

Andrew Marvell: a collection of critical essays, ed. by G. de F. Lord, New Jersey, 1968 (*Twentieth Century Views*).

Andrew Marvell: a critical anthology, ed. by John Carey, 1969 (*Penguin Critical Anthologies*).

Marvell: modern judgements, by Michael Wilding, 1969.

Collections of essays on Marvell are to be published during 1978 by the Universities of Hull (ed. by R. L. Brett) and York (ed. by C. A. Patrides).

Bibliographies of research

In Pierre Legouis, *André Marvell*, 1928 (see above), pp.471–87.

Andrew Marvell 1927–1967, ed. by Dennis G. Donovan, 1969 (*Elizabethan Bibliographies Supplements*).

The New Cambridge Bibliography of English Literature, ed. by G. Watson, Cambridge, 1974, vol. 1, cols. 1222–1229.

Gillian Szanto, 'Recent Studies in Marvell', *English Literary Renaissance*, V (1975), 273–82.

Note: Brief reviews of articles and longer works are to be found in *The Year's Work in English Studies* published in Britain by the English Association, and in the *Annual Bibliography of English Language and Literature* published by the Modern Humanities Research Association. Of several purely enumerative lists the Modern Language Association of America's *Bibliography of Books and Articles on the Modern Languages and Literatures*, issued annually, is perhaps the most comprehensive.

NOTE

The following items are represented in the exhibition by photographs: numbers 6, 8, 11, 13, 15, 21, 27, 32, 40, 42, 45, 58, 62, 64, 74, 80, 81, 83, 88, 97, 110 and 113.